Master the Art of Data Storytelling with Visualizations

Alexander N. Donovan

Funny helpful tips:

Engage with online forums and discussions; they offer diverse interpretations and insights on books.

Stay committed to ethical sourcing; it enhances brand image and sustainability.

Master the Art of Data Storytelling with Visualizations : Master the Art of Effective Data Communication & Engage Your Audience with this Comprehensive Guide

Life advices:

Challenge yourself with complex texts; they stimulate cognitive growth and critical thinking.

Practice patience; understanding takes time and effort.

Introduction

This is your gateway to the dynamic world of data, stories, and narratives. This comprehensive guide offers insights and techniques to help you make sense of data, transform it into compelling stories, and create impactful visualizations.

The journey begins with an exploration of the fundamental concepts, including the nature of data, the distinction between data and wisdom, and the role of narratives and stories in conveying information effectively. Drawing inspiration from Aristotle, you'll delve into the ethical dimensions of storytelling, ensuring your narratives are not only informative but also responsible.

The guide goes on to uncover the essential elements of effective visualization, equipping you with the knowledge and tools needed to craft visuals that resonate with your audience. Engaging quizzes and practical case studies, such as storytelling climate change and visualizing gender, provide hands-on learning experiences.

To ensure the integrity of your visualizations, you'll discover how to conduct chart due diligence, navigate the influence of gravity on data presentation, and explore mental frameworks that enhance your understanding of complex information.

The guide also delves into the journey from knowledge to wisdom, offering a case study on innovation policy in Singapore and insights into using rankings for situational awareness. You'll learn how to identify and address bias in data, ensuring your visualizations are accurate and impartial.

As you progress through the guide, you'll gain valuable tips and techniques for decluttering various chart types, using personas to connect with your audience, visualizing differences effectively, and putting global financial data into perspective.

This book is designed to empower individuals and professionals alike to harness the power of data, storytelling, and visualization. Whether you're a data enthusiast, journalist, educator, or business leader, this guide equips you with the skills and knowledge to transform raw data into meaningful narratives and visuals that inform, inspire, and engage.

Contents

CHAPTER 1 DATA, STORIES & NARRATIVES

Fig 1 *These three magazines publish some of the most influential charts on the newsstand. Did you know that none of them is made with Excel?* [5]

BEFORE YOU START

Before visualizing, there is data. However, before working with data it is important to understand what knowledge is. What is knowledge to you? In this chapter, you will learn three things: (i) the **difference** between data, information, and knowledge, (ii) what **wisdom** is, and (iii) what the **process** to produce knowledge is.

WHAT IS DATA?

Exercise: Order the words

What is data to you? We always open data visualization workshops with this exercise.

Consider the following ideas

knowledge

data

wisdom

information

Now, order them as logically as possible

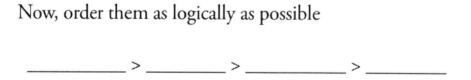

Fig 2 *An exercise to understand what data is by relating it to knowledge.*

Data has many definitions. However, to understand, there's nothing like doing an exercise. There are various ways to learn something. By listening, by talking about it, by reading about it and, by doing it. Of those four, doing has the highest recall rate. Can you order the four words (data knowledge information wisdom)? Most students will come up with the following ordering:

data *> information > knowledge >* ***wisdom***

Once the order of the words has been agreed upon, we can discuss the ordering criteria. Why did we order them the way we did? This is a great conversation starter. To ground the conversation, it further helps to list the attributes of the words at the extremes. What are the attributes that **distinguish** data vs. wisdom?

DATA VS. WISDOM

Exercise: Compare the concepts

Given this ordering,

Data > Information > Knowledge > Wisdom;

Write three adjectives that best describe each

Data   Wisdom

_____   _____

_____   _____

_____   _____

Fig 3 *An exercise used to understand the arrow of value between data and wisdom.*

Solution

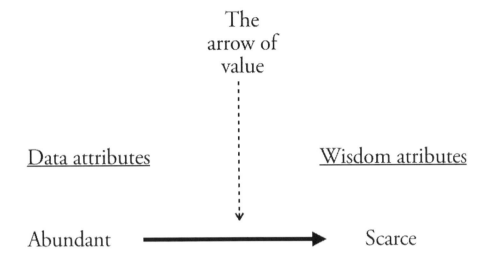

Fig 4 *The arrow of value.*

Data is **many** while wisdom is usually characterized by **few**. Data is abundant, wisdom is scarce. Value is closely correlated with scarcity too. This exercise is great to clarify the pervasive confusion between data, information, knowledge, and its relationship to value, scarcity, and wisdom.

WHAT IS WISDOM?
The synthesis process

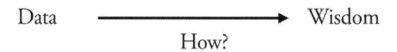

Fig 5 *This arrow represents a process.*

Jackie Chan says in one of his films, "information is not knowledge, and knowledge is not wisdom". But what is wisdom? Is wisdom just knowledge in context? Is wisdom meta knowledge? — knowledge about knowledge? And more importantly, knowing in which situation to apply a given knowledge? Even if the definition is not universal, what we are more interested in here is how to transform knowledge into wisdom. Why? Because it is a high added value activity and one of the reasons (if not the only reason) why companies employ data scientists. One way to arrive at wisdom is the **Synthesis process** — the dialectic combination of thesis and antithesis into a higher truth.

Exercise: match the words with Lego

Connect each keyword with its corresponding image. Time 1 minute.

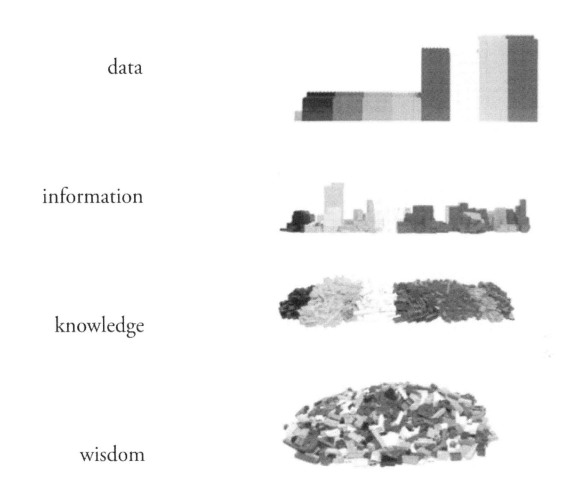

data

information

knowledge

wisdom

Fig 6 *An exercise used to understand what wisdom is. Lego image source: LinkedIn, anonymous 'meme'.*

Solution

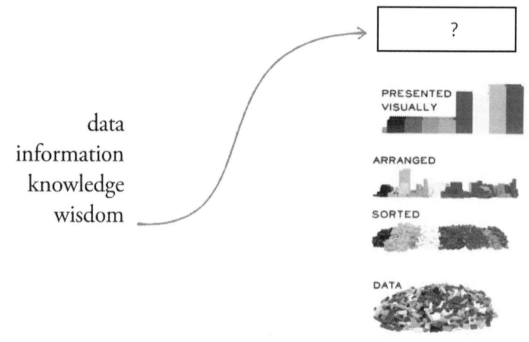

Fig 7 *To solve this exercise, think outside of the box.*

In this exercise, students must match the words to a Lego configuration. Each Lego piece represents some piece of data. The Lego exercise is a great way to clarify that wisdom (and to some extent knowledge) is **not** just data arranged and visually presented. Let us zoom into this case. Imagine you are the C.E.O. of Lego and this information has been presented to you. Can you map the words to the pictures? Where does wisdom map to?

In this exercise, wisdom is orphan to drive home the point that wisdom is something more than presenting and arranging data. In other words, wisdom is knowing where to **apply** knowledge. Example of wisdom: "We do not have any pink Lego pieces in this set. Why is this? Are we blind to some important customer segment? Are sales not optimal because of that?" Note how valuable knowledge emerges when we connect our information (there are no pink bricks) to other existing knowledge (gender studies).

INFORMATION VS. MEANING

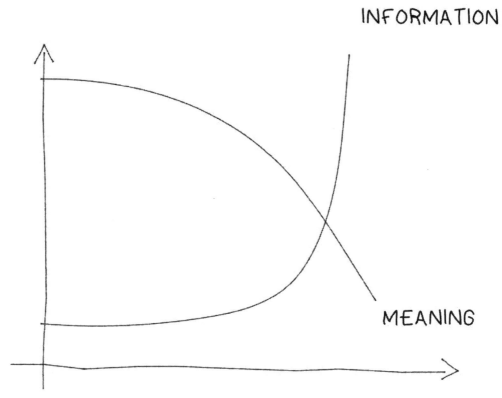

INFORMATION

MEANING

Fig 8 *"There is no peace in more".*

Meaning vs. Information

A version of this chart was originally posted by Hugh McLeod, the author of "Ignore Everybody". When I first saw this chart, I felt mesmerized by it. Then I tried to find flaws in the chart. But there are no flaws. This chart is a masterpiece. I was just flummoxed at the simplicity of it[6]. The y-axis is the amount of information, (See Shannon Information Entropy). It can be measured in bits. The x-axis is an ordinal sequence (not continuous, and has no units). It is an ordering of cases (for example they could be charts or visualization examples) that the author ranked in descending order of **meaning** along the x-axis; for each element, two dots on the y-axis are plotted. Then the author drinks his own medicine and simplifies the chart to reduce all non-essential information to deliver the *Aha* moment: Less (info) is more (meaning). The INFORMATION - labeled line is sometimes called the hockey stick. It is an exponential function. The MEANING- line fits a downward parabola. What this chart means is that it is **not** possible to have meaning with information overload.

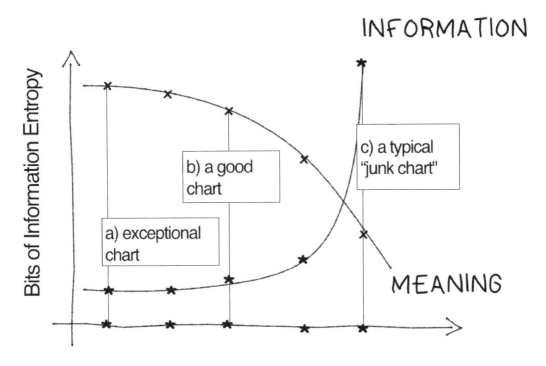

Fig 9 *A scientific deconstruction of McLeod's chart.*

Exercise: summarize the previous 20 pages

Summarize the previous 20 pages in 20 words or less. Time 3 minutes.

Now, visualize it

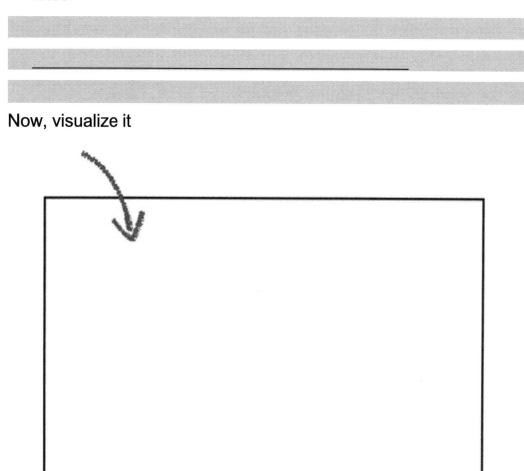

Solution

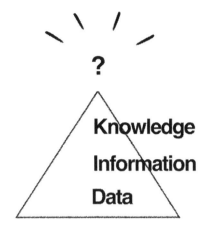

Fig 10 *A visual metaphor based on the DIKW model.*

Wrapping-up

When delivering a workshop, this exercise is a great way to bring attention to the point of **summary** vs. **synthesis**. A summary is a mere reduction process whereas synthesis is <u>**demonstrating**</u> an understanding of the subject by relating it to other subjects, ultimately adding and generating new knowledge or ideas through <u>**connective thinking**</u>. In Fig 10, we summarized the relationship between data and wisdom by way of the pyramid **metaphor**. Elements at the top of the pyramid are valuable, scarce, and hard to carry to the top because they work against the force of **gravity**. This is a great example of a visual summary of the chapter while also a good example of synthesis.

Now that we've learned the difference between data, information, knowledge, and how to transform knowledge into wisdom, let's look at the role of narratives in charts.

NARRATIVES & STORIES

Exercise: fill the gap with a verb

Fill in the blank with a verb. Example: "Data_____stories". Time 3 minutes.

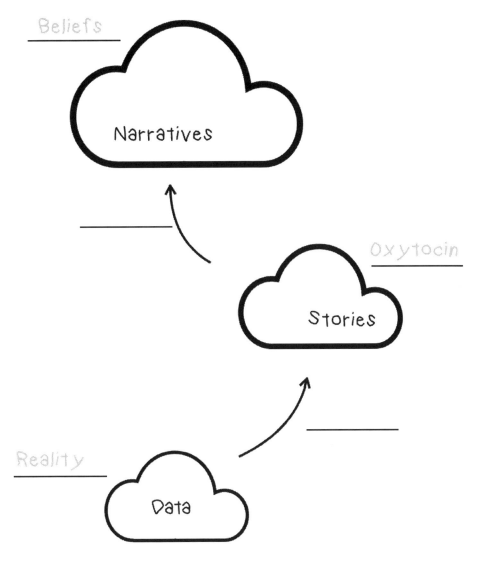

Fig 11 *An exercise used to understand the difference between narratives and stories.*

Solution

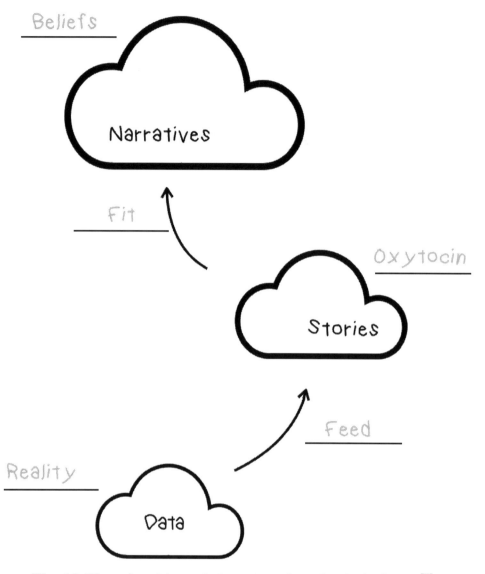

Beliefs

Narratives

Fit

Oxytocin

Stories

Feed

Reality

Data

Fig 12 *The cloud template, use when logic is fuzzy[7].*

The role of tales in our culture

To understand what a narrative is, we first need to understand what a story is. A story is an account of events. We, humans, love stories. Why? Telling and consuming stories is addictive. For example, listening to an Aesop fable, reading a book, and watching a movie, all those release oxytocin in the brain— the feel-good hormone. That is why people get addicted to Netflix, Venezuelan soap operas, and fiction books. Oral storytelling is thought to be the earliest method for sharing narratives. From an anthropological perspective, during most childhoods, narratives are used to shape children on proper behavior and values. This is usually done through tales.

Narratives

A narrative is a set of beliefs, values, or *worldview*. Therefore, the chosen narrative **interprets** the story (and consequently the underlying data/reality). An example of a narrative popular in European culture is that kids, especially young girls, should not trust strangers. A story that promotes that narrative is the story of the

Little Red Riding Hood, a tale from the 10th Century. In fables, a narrative is also made explicit at the end of the tale as in the moral of the story. The difference between the moral of the story and a narrative is of the context of use. The moral of the story is associated with fables for kids while narratives are associated with "shaping" public opinion and mass media (See Burson-Marsteller & Co.). An example of a well-known narrative is **FUD** — Fear, Uncertainty, and Doubt. It is also known as a disinformation

strategy[8] used to thwart change to the status quo. It is said that IBM was one of the first companies listed on the Dow Jones to use FUD openly. An exemplification was, "*Nobody gets fired for buying an IBM*".

CONNECTION TO ARISTOTLE

Because the goal of a story is to persuade; narratives, stories, and data are related to the three modes of persuasion of Aristotle — The

Ethos, the *Pathos,* and the *Logos*[9]. The narrative is related to the Ethos (to appeal to the ethical values). The story is related to Pathos (to appeal to the emotions). The data that supports the story is related to the Logos (to appeal to logic).

Exercise: Brexit bus

Identify the **narrative**, the **story**, the **data**, and the **call to action** in this photo. Time 2 minutes.

Fig 13 A Brexit Bus, UK. Original photo by David Beeson.

Solution

Fig 14 *Annotations by a student.*

At first glance, the Brexit bus story is an example of a narrative where an out-group steals from an in-group. But it is more than that. In fact, the bus appeals to so many people because it is connected to four narratives:

1)   Appeal to in-group tribal instincts to fight "outsiders"

2) Doing for the common good is ethical
3) Fighting unfairness is ethical too
4) Maximizing the utility of a resource is common sense.

These narratives were brilliantly embodied in the Brexit bus. The statistics and words printed on the bus were later found to be lies, but it did not matter. This story checked all the boxes of the pro-Brexit voters and mobilized them.

IS YOUR NARRATIVE ETHICAL?

Any narrative can be evaluated from an ethical perspective. There are four ethical frameworks[10] commonly used to evaluate. Each one maximizes some different ethical criteria. For each framework, the most ethical choice is the one that maximizes a different policy.

The four frameworks

1) In the so-called Utilitarian framework, the most ethical choice is the one that optimizes global happiness.
2) In the Common good framework, the most ethical choice is the one that optimizes the Well-being of society.
3) In the Fairness framework, the most ethical choice is the one that optimizes equity.
4) In the Virtues framework, the most ethical choice is the one that aligns best with a set of predefined values.

Equity vs. equality

Fig 15 *Equity is not the same as equality. "Interaction Institute for Social Change". Source: Angus Maguire.*

Examples of famous virtue frameworks

1) Liberté, égalité, fraternité[11]
2) The ten commandments
3) The Bushido – the way of the warrior
4) Mr. Miyagi, Karate Kid

What are ethical dilemmas?

The so-called ethical dilemmas arise when a conflict between the approaches appears. Besides, dilemmas can also arise when different regions in the brain (amygdala vs. frontal lobe) evaluate a situation with opposed outcomes. (See Trolley dilemma[12]).

Choices & ethics

To be ethical one needs to first consider at least two choices. Many times, we end up with suboptimal choices simply because alternatives were not even considered. Before disseminating a visual, always consider **two** alternatives. Then apply an appropriate framework to rank the alternatives. (If something goes wrong at least you can show you followed a process).

ELEMENTS OF EFFECTIVE VISUALIZATION

Exercise: the plane visual

Summarize the relationship between story, narrative, and data in the visual below that is titled **Elements of effective visualization**. The visual uses a plane as a powerful storytelling metaphor. Fill in the gaps. Time 3 minutes.

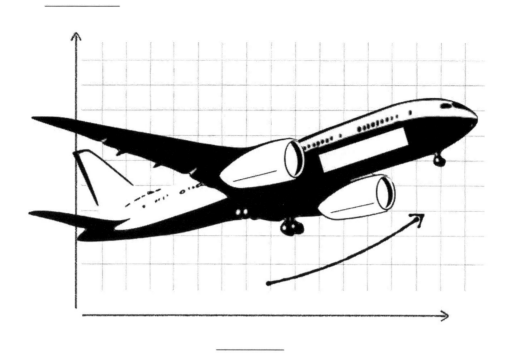

Fig 16 Visual metaphors + annotations, so powerful. (Solution on the next page)

Solution

Effective

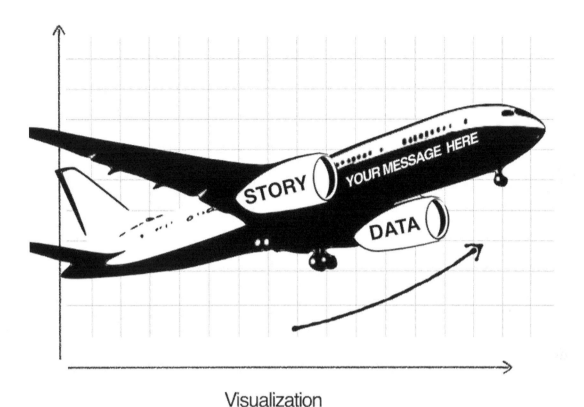

Visualization

Fig 17 *Never let technical words like 'narrative' get in the way of a great story.*

Interpretation: according to this visual, to persuade others effectively we need:

- A *why* or a narrative ("your message here," is the *payload*, you are the pilot)

- A **story** (to 'transport' the payload)

- **Data** (to 'power' the credibility of the story)

QUIZ: NARRATIVES & STORIES

True or False? Time 5 minutes.

1) A story is an account of events. [True / False]
2) Story consumption releases oxytocin. [T/F]
3) The purpose of a story is to advocate (transmit, perpetuate) a narrative (a belief, a culture, an ideology). [T/F]
4) A narrative does not stick to the human brain, it cannot go viral, it is not easy to remember. [T/F]
5) If your story (chart, visualization) advocates for no narrative, it will feel like it has no purpose. [T/F]

(Solution on the next page)

Solution

1) A story is an account of events [T/F]. True. To gain perspective on this question also see Lisa Feldman's work on the Constructed Model of the World as Reality.
2) Story consumption releases oxytocin [T/F]. True. To learn more, check the biochemistry of storytelling and its function in evolution.
3) The purpose of a story is to advocate (transmit, perpetuate) a narrative (a belief, a culture, an ideology) [T/F]. True.
4) A narrative does not stick to the human brain, it cannot go viral, it is not easy to remember [T/F]. True. The message of a narrative in its succinct form is usually not viral. Stories in form of Ads, movies, and books are more suited to go viral.
5) If your story (chart, visualization) advocates for no narrative, it will feel like it has no purpose [T/F]. True.

CASE: STORYTELLING CLIMATE CHANGE

Time 15 minutes. Online search: allowed. In August 2019 Greta Thunberg set sail from Europe to a UN climate conference on the other side of the Atlantic. Identify the data, the story, and the narrative in this story.

Fig 18 *Unlike Al Gore in 2006, Greta Thunberg needed no charts to get her message across* [13].

A solution to Storytelling climate change

Narratives (example of answers)

1) The underdog wins[14]
2) Role reversal
3) Dysfunctional family
4) Climate change is an emergency

Story

"You might be grown-ups but you are not mature enough to understand this emergency. If you did, you would not jet to the conference as you do. You could Skype, or travel like me to reduce your carbon footprint. Hence, you (not me) are behaving like the immature kid." See the abridged speech[15].

Data

1) Look at the big waves behind me, I am serious, this is dangerous
2) A carbon-neutral sail-ship = it's possible to reduce the carbon footprint
3) The situation is bad enough that I had to skip school classes
4) Air jet-set travel produces CO_2 but there are alternatives look at me

How to transform Data into Information

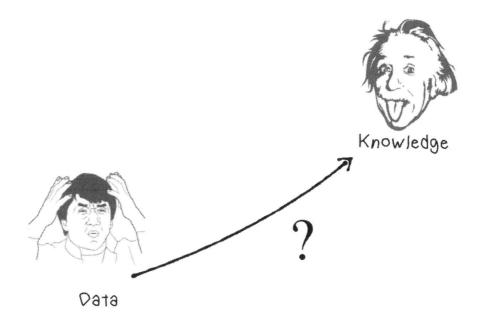

Knowledge

Data

Fig 19 *Creating knowledge from data, the secret to winning the Nobel prize?*[16]

In this chapter, you will learn to transform data into information, (a prerequisite to produce knowledge). In other words, how to make your charts more useful by displaying information **effectively**.

"The foundation of a useful chart is seldom graphic design"

The bulk of published books on data visualization focus on how to build charts and how to make them readable. A few of them spend a considerable number of pages listing all the types of charts available out there and use the good chart / bad chart template to teach how a little tweak can make or break the readability of a chart.

Others give color advice and how important it is not to clutter your chart with colors, (see also the term *junkcharts* coined by Tufte). This helps improve readability and aesthetics but it is not so helpful in transforming information into knowledge, the previous step before wisdom, and prescriptive analytics. And while poor color choices can kill the readability of any chart, focusing on chart aestheticism is the equivalent to teaching about the importance of font types to someone that just wants to become a writer. After all, the book Harry Potter did not become a bestseller because of the font type they used. In the same vein, the typical root cause of a poor chart is not design but failing to transform data into (meaningful) knowledge.

Let's see an example of how to transform information into knowledge with data from a gender distribution survey in STEM.

VISUALIZING GENDER

Exercise: Visualize gender

How would you **visualize** the following gender breakdown of data scientists? Time 3 minutes.

Survey responses	
Female	16.8%
Male	81.4%
NS	1.4%
ND	0.3%

Solution

Solution with Matplotlib

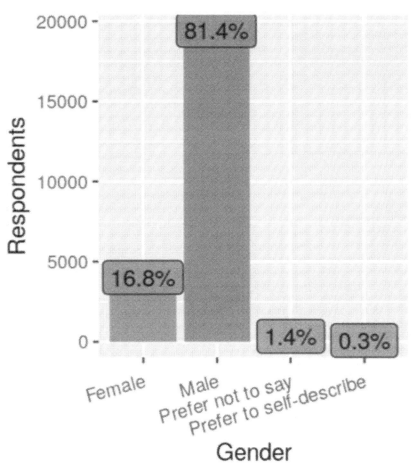

Fig 20 *This default Matplotlib chart uses* **four** *different font sizes and* **six** *colors (see* <u>slides</u>*). If you are watching this on a Kindle or the paperback edition you will be seeing six shades of gray instead.*

Exercise: Discriminate the types of information

Is the figure above data, information, or knowledge? Why? Reason your answer. Time 2 minutes.

Solution

It is just information. We did not create knowledge by producing this chart. It is not knowledge because it is **not** *more* useful than the original raw data. IT is not faster to read either. A final criticism of this visual is the information overload. To display just four data points we have used six shades or colors with little justification.

Reflection

Unless you are in a preliminary Exploratory Data Analysis (EDA), it is not a good idea to disseminate a chart unless there is a clear why (narrative) for the chart. And even if you produce many charts as a part of an EDA, resist the temptation to show them off. In this case, we are asked to visualize the gender distribution of the members of a data science website [27]. Gender was one of the questions in the survey which was answered by about 30k data scientists. Fig 20, is the default settings chart produced using the popular python library *Matplotlib*. This chart is perfectly fine. It is informative, but there is no message, there is no why. It lacks a purpose. Why?

One reason is that it is **not** connected to any narrative. Another reason is that it does not increase our knowledge. Is it helping us to become wiser? Is it facilitating the prescriptive analytics function? How would you make this chart more useful?

Exercise: Draw three alternatives

Draw here at least **three** alternative charts to Fig 20? Time 3 minutes. (Solution on the next page).

THE CHART-NARRATIVE FIT

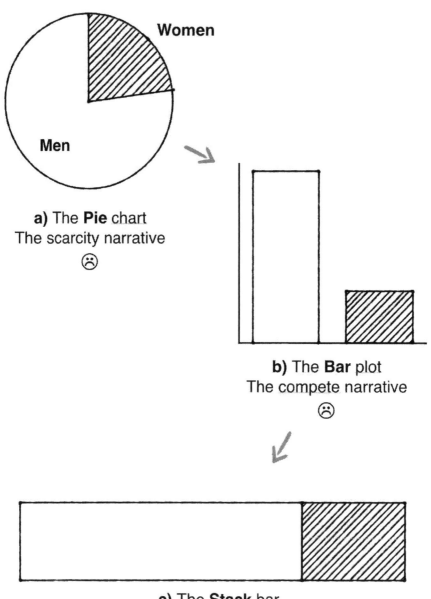

a) The **Pie** chart
The scarcity narrative
☹

b) The **Bar** plot
The compete narrative
☹

c) The **Stack** bar
Gravity neutral, growth-mindset narrative
☺

Fig 21 *Three ways to visualize the same data.*

Choosing the right chart

Fig 21 shows the same information as Fig 20 in three different ways,

a) pie chart

b) bar chart

c) stack bar chart horizontal

Let's consider the process we followed to produce them.

Simplify

We consider men and women only and ignore the other two outlier groups. Why? We can choose to include the 1% of respondents that identified as outliers. However, as we mentioned in the death by PowerPoint section, it is best to focus on one idea per chart, not two. If we want to talk about outliers then it is better to do so in a dedicated chart. Always follow the idea of one idea per chart!

Avoid overload of colors

In Fig 21, the men are represented in white and the women in the dashed area. We avoided color because we can. Colors are loaded with symbolisms[17], shades of greys less so. Conjugating colors is a very subtle art that is easy to underestimate. Why use more than two colors without proper graphic design training? We have also removed the scales, figures, and axis labels. We traded off a bit of accuracy for a big gain in clarity.

Consider a narrative

Let's assume we are advocating for a gender equity narrative. We define the equity narrative as a world view in which the world will be a better place if there is less gender ratio imbalance[18].

Check the chart-narrative fit

Once a narrative is set, choosing a **compatible** chart template is the next step to transform information into knowledge. In this case, pies and bars are a poor choice. Why? Because pie charts are connected to the narrative of how much pie each kid gets (finite resources, fights), it is a confrontational narrative that undermines the narrative of gender equity.

The bar plot chart is also a poor choice because it is connected to the narrative of competing and to other win-lose narratives such as scarcity and the view that men and women compete. Using them

risks undermining any growth mindset[19] or equity (win-win) narrative that you might be advocating for. The stacked bar is a better choice. It is horizontal so it is not subject to the gravity metaphor. (See gravity & charts). Now that we have found a fit between the chart and the narrative, let's design the chart in ways that are easier to assimilate by humans. We call these charts **human-centered** charts. Human-centered charts leverage the same principles as human-centered design by placing the user at the center of the design process.

HUMAN-CENTERED CHARTS

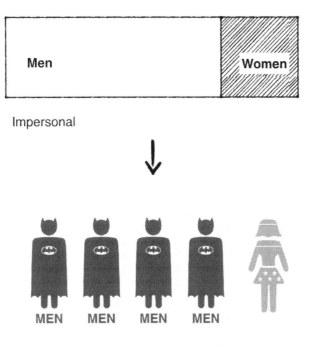

Impersonal

MEN   MEN   MEN   MEN

Human centric

Fig 22 *Four Batmen and a Wonder woman make this chart easier to remember.*

Using superheroes is one way to visualize the heavy[20] topic of gender equity in STEM environments. We also use the iso-measure. In an iso-measure chart, each unit (in this case a superhero icon) represents the same quantity (in this case, about 5,000 respondents of the survey). We also reduced the superhero count to the minimum possible (five persons) which means we approximate the original percentages to a 1:4 female to male ratio. This chart can also be read as follows: on average, for every 5 people in a team (room, meeting, office), one will be female.

Checking the chart-narrative fit

Given the same gender equity narrative used earlier, let's see how the design choices we made fit such narrative.

1) A superhero's job is to make the world a better place, the equity narrative is about making the world a better place
2) The iso-measure is humans, like the respondents
3) The number of heroes is less than seven, (we are respecting the 7 chunks rule and not overloading the reader with information)
4) We use humor[21] to improve memorability

Leveraging humor

Many charts are impersonal because we cannot relate to them. We solved that with the superheroes. See also user personas in Ch. 6. However, if besides we want the audience to remember the chart, we can use humor or an insider joke as in, data scientists *are* superheroes because they have to "wrangle" with data, see the term *data wrangling.*

Tableau

Brian Sedaca, a visualizer from Argentina, shares his version of this exercise using Tableau "public" at _Gender Gap visualizations that fit your Narratives_.[22]

"It was insightful to read about the relationships between the different visualization options and the narrative we intend to support in the first edition of this book. The excitement of grasping new knowledge moved me to action: I had to replicate it in Tableau…"

Tableau is a powerful data visualization tool. The one that best supports the visualizer in following the precepts of data visualizations best practices. I am sure you can replicate this work with the tool of your choice (Excel, Power BI, Spotfire, etc.), but it is just faster with Tableau as the default settings are closer to best practices.

One of the great things about Tableau, is "Tableau Public". It gives access to tons of great data visualizations and dashboards from all over the world in any topics you can imagine. There you can access the dashboard as well as the individual worksheets that compose it. This allows to reverse engineer any visualization (including this one) and to adapt it to your own use case.

SEXISM IN YOUR CHART?

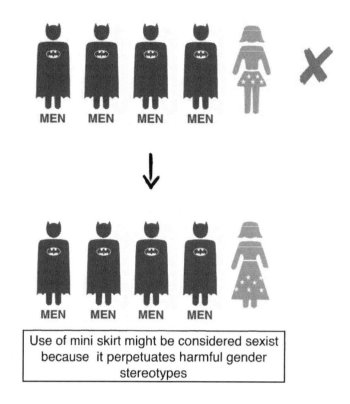

Use of mini skirt might be considered sexist because it perpetuates harmful gender stereotypes

Fig 23 *Always check for blind spots.*

CHART DUE DILIGENCE CHECKLIST

☑ Type of chart compatible with the narrative (message)

☑ No color overload (3 colors max)

☑ One chart, one message

☑ Metaphors aligned with the narrative

☑ I don't need to read the caption to understand the chart

☑ The caption is used as a synthesis opportunity

☑ The caption does not explain the chart again

☑ Bias checked by a third party

It is important to check for blind spots. Charts are no different. It is prudent to ask for a bias check to a diversity of people, ideally with different backgrounds. See Chapter 5 for more on *bias*.

GRAVITY & CHARTS

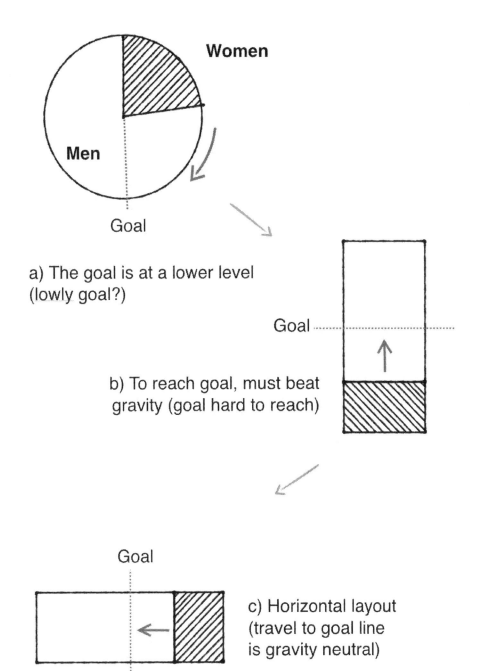

Women

Men

Goal

a) The goal is at a lower level (lowly goal?)

Goal

b) To reach goal, must beat gravity (goal hard to reach)

Goal

c) Horizontal layout (travel to goal line is gravity neutral)

How gravity affects goals

Let's assume your charts have convinced your organization that achieving gender parity at work is a good goal and after a board meeting a goal of reaching a 50% female to male ratio has been set. How to visualize it to **persuade** and rally the rest of the organization? The arrows point to the goal. Note how the alignment of the arrows with the direction of gravity influences how the goal achievability is perceived. In the pie chart, the downward arrow has a negative connotation. For the vertical stack bar, the upward arrow against gravity makes the goal appear hard to achieve. The horizontal stack bar is gravity neutral and the freest of connotations that might distract from the narrative.

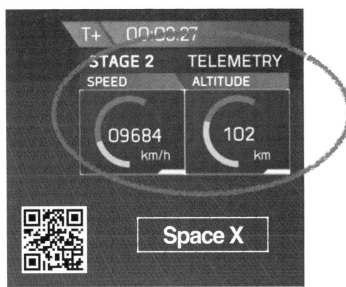

Fig 25 Musk vs. Bezos. Two visions of space exploration. Two ways to visualize altitude.

There is a fundamental difference between circular charts and bar charts. The brain is sensitive to angular change and (by comparison) quite numb to linear change[23]. This is particularly true when considering motion, and sensitivity to small changes. If in your narrative, highlighting minute changes in a variable is important for the story, then circular pie charts (speed needle gauges) are the way to go. If on the contrary, too much attention to change is a distraction, avoid pie charts and needles. Compare for yourself. In the Blue origin videocast, the attitude change is barely noticeable. Whereas in the *SpaceX* cast, it pops during all the cast.

1) Blue Origin cast: http://bit.ly/2NHycmf
2) SpaceX cast: http://bit.ly/2XwXYxY

QUIZ: MAKING USEFUL CHARTS

True or False? Time 10 minutes.

1) A bar chart is a great way to visualize the odds of the Casino Roulette. [T/F]
2) Humans are more sensitive to pie charts than bar charts. However, in animated charts where the ratios change, these changes are more obvious in a bar chart. [T/F]
3) A drawback of the iso-measure chart is that one cannot use metaphors or personas with it. [T/F]
4) A way to turn information into knowledge is to use a palette with the minimum amount of colors possible. [T/F]
5) The purpose of an EDA is to tell a story about the data. [T/F]

(Solution on the next page)

Solution

1) A bar chart is a great way to visualize the odds of the Casino Roulette [T/ **F**]. **False**. A bar chart is linked to the competition narrative. The roulette is a zero-sum game. A Pie chart, an **iso-measure** chart, or a photo of the roulette itself communicates odds more clearly.

2) Humans are more sensitive to pie charts than bar charts. However, in animated charts where the ratios change, those changes are more obvious in a bar chart. [T/F]. **False**. They are more sensitive to pies/ needles in **both** situations.

3) A drawback of the iso-measure chart is that one cannot use metaphors or personas with it. [T/F]. **False**. It is the **opposite**. The iso-measure lends itself to metaphors.

4) A way to turn information into knowledge is to use a palette with the minimum amount of colors possible [T/F]. **False**. **Avoiding** information overload is a pre-condition for knowledge. However, the fundamental transform is usefulness. (Usually, by connecting it to other knowledge).

5) The purpose of an EDA is to tell a story about the data [T/F]. **False**. The **main** purpose of an Exploratory Data Analysis is to aggregate and visualize basic statistical information.

CHAPTER 3 KNOWLEDGE

How to create knowledge?

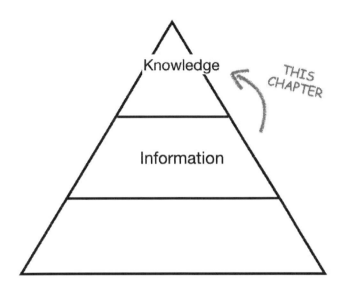

Knowledge

THIS CHAPTER

Information

Fig 26 *This chart uses the gravity metaphor.*

In Chapter 1, we saw that charts with purpose have a *message*. In Chapter 2, we saw an example of how to transform gender data into information. In this chapter, we will learn how to synthesize information into knowledge. If we were in high school, this would be the equivalent of analyzing a text and then writing the synthesis. Your data is the text; the chart with valuable insights is the synthesis. An effective way to do this is by using reference frameworks, summarization techniques, and visual metaphors. Let's see an example that uses age data from the previous survey.

MENTAL FRAMEWORKS

Let's take a look at the chart in Fig 27. How many chunks of information can you count? It has information overload. Let's focus on the color palette, for instance, a rainbow. However, a rainbow does not convey any useful meaning here. On the contrary, by using 12 colors, (12 shades of gray if you are on a Kindle), we have increased the information overload by a whopping **12 memory chunks** with a **zero** gain in meaning. See also information vs. meaning in Chapter 1.

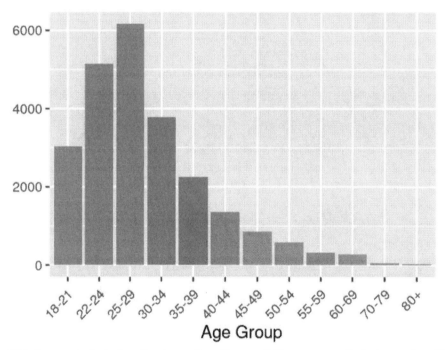

Fig 27 A ggplot default visualization of the age of data scientists. Source: the Kaggle 2018 survey [27].

Exercise: make the histogram more useful

How would you make the previous chart more **useful**? We can start by reducing the information overload! Draw solutions. Time 2 minutes.

Solution

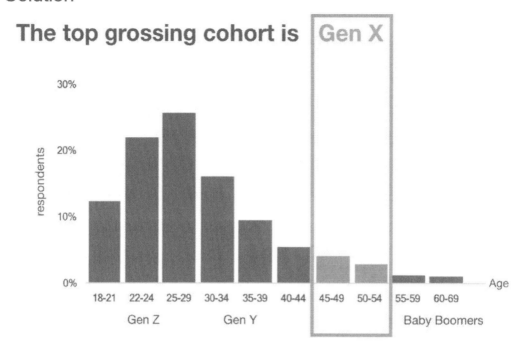

Fig 28 *Same information with a narrative, and linked to a reference framework becomes closer to knowledge.*

What can we learn from senior data scientists?

Like Fig 27, Fig 28 is user distribution by age too. However, here we use a two-color scheme to highlight which age group won the most competitions per user. However, just a few too many age bins can overwhelm any reader. A way to declutter and structure the bins into **usable** information is to reduce their numbers and group them in a familiar, relatable form. One way to do this is to reduce age groups to generation groups. In this case, we used a reference framework many are familiar with: Generations in the workforce. It comprises

the gen X, Y, Z, and the Boomers[24]. Furthermore, we are interested to see which group is the most productive in terms of competitions and cash prizes per user. Because everyone belongs to a generation this chart can become very personable. What can we learn from the wisdom that each generation offers? Source: 2018 Kaggle Survey Q2 What is your age?

Generation & work-ethic attribute framework

1) The **Baby Boomers**, born 1946 – 1964, "often branded workaholics[25]"
2) **Gen X**, born 1967 – 1977, "this generation works to live and carry with them a level of cynicism"
3) **Gen Y**, "Millennials" born 1980 – 2000, "considered the most educated and self-aware generation in employment"
4) **Gen Z**[26], born after 2000

Narrative

Ageism is the narrative that says things like "old people do not have the energy to be entrepreneurial and cannot innovate"[27]. However, a few papers [28] have disproved this claim. The chart advocates for the opposite narrative, "(in data science), older generations are as productive as younger generations".

Knowledge creation

Note how the key step to creating meaning (knowledge) is not only to summarize and declutter but to find **where** the information is most useful and then by linking it to **that** context (reference framework). In this case, (i) Generations in the workplace, and (ii) productivity. Another way to create meaning and storytelling at the same time is by way of visual metaphors such as the pyramid. Next, let's see a stunning example based on salary distribution.

VISUALIZING INCLUSION

Yearly salary in USD

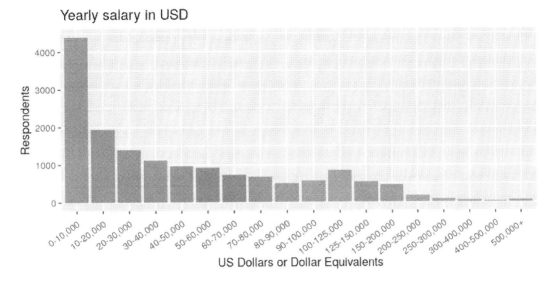

Fig 29 *A default ggplot2 visualization of the salaries of data scientists. Source: Kaggle 2018 Survey. Source Q9 What is your current yearly compensation.*

Exercise: Transform this information into knowledge

In the previous section, we saw an example of **meaning** created by way of connecting information to a reference framework. Now let's do the same and, in addition, let's apply a visual metaphor. Let's look at salary data from the same 2018 survey. Is Fig 29 data information or knowledge?

Given an inclusion narrative, how would you create a more useful chart? Time 6 minutes. Hint: If the chart was a building where would highly paid individuals own apartments?

Intermediate step

(Fig 29 rotated counter-clockwise 90 degrees)

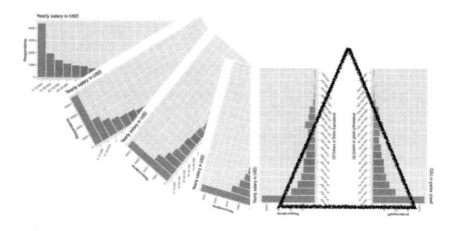

Fig 30 *Does your chart fit any visual metaphor?*

Solution

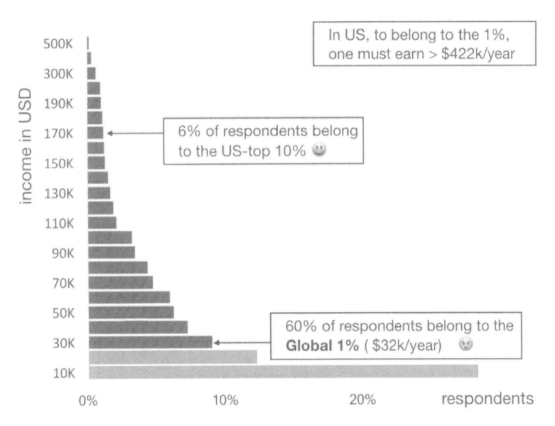

Fig 31 *Using text inside charts is a great way to defuse ambiguity.*

Earlier we mentioned the importance of the chart-narrative fit. Fig 31's narrative is about the digital divide. How inclusive is data science as a community? As we just saw in the previous section, one way to create knowledge is to relate our information to existing reference frameworks. Generations in the workforce is an example of a popular framework to think about age and workforce.

Helping the reader **situate** the new information into existing frameworks makes the new information easier to assimilate, use and recall. Here, we apply the reference framework of *income percentiles* – a common analysis framework used by economists and fit it with the pyramid a metaphor that represents hierarchies. See also the #onepercent movement. In the US, to belong to the 1% elite, one needs to earn more than $422k per year[29]. About 23 respondents declared that they do. In addition, about 6% declared they belong to the 10% percentile, a very inclusive number because 6% is similar to 10%.

The 10% percentile income is about $166k in the US[30], so if the sample reflects the distribution found in society, it means it is at least somehow inclusive. We add a smiley emoji to reassure the reader that yes, this is good. However, those numbers are for US household incomes. When we look globally, the 1% percentile threshold is $32k per year.

This puts 60% of the respondents in the top 1%. 60% is very different from 1%, so globally this data point does not support inclusiveness because it does not reflect the global distribution. Aha moment. One way to create such moments in the story is to A/Bify the story by switching between two points of view. We just saw how powerful visual metaphors can be. Let's see three more examples.

WINNER TAKES ALL

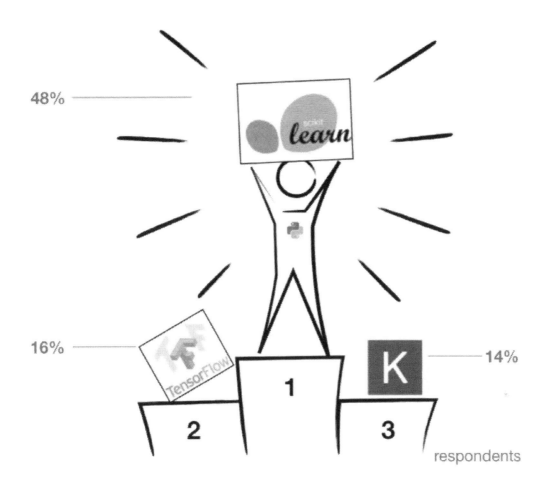

48% ------

16% ------

14%

1

2

3

respondents

Fig 32 *The top three ML libraries.*

Here, we are visualizing the data science libraries the respondents use. Using the same survey, *Question 20: Of the choices that you selected in the previous question, which ML library have you used the most?* Given a winner takes all narrative (so common in the software world), what visual metaphor can we apply? This chart is an example of less is more. In this case, Sci-Kit (a famous scientific Python library) has a 48% share, Google's TensorFlow has a 16%, followed by Keras 14%. Let's see how this visual is connected to the narrative.

Chart-narrative fit

In scenarios with strong network externalities at play such as social network, a phone OS, or an Olympic race; being on the podium (being first) has a disproportionate effect on the reward. In such cases, the winner-takes-all narrative is in place. Anthropomorphizing the ranking with a podium conveys a memorable narrative and affordance — the glory the winner deserves for the great utility this library provided to the community. This narrative is also connected to other memes famous in the software world such as the developer's glory. (See S. Balmer in "Developers, developers, developers, developers").

ALL OR NOTHING

In the previous section, we visualized data about the most popular ML libraries with a winner takes all narrative, here we do the same with a different narrative.

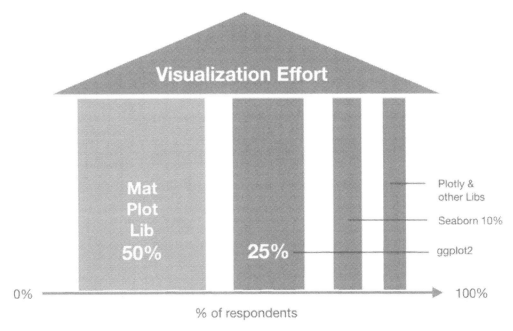

Fig 33 *The house of Shiva. When colored areas occupy large areas, use 50% grey and pastel colors instead of 100% solid bold colors.*

House of Shiva

Fig 33 is a combination of, (i) a chart template called Marimekko, with (ii) a symbolic chart called *House of Shiva*.

The House of Shiva is used to emphasize all or nothing relations. The metaphor is that the roof falls if just one column collapses.

Symbolism

The columns support the visualization efforts of the community (roof load, common good). The width of the "columns" expresses how much work/load each column supports. Grey columns on the right represent other less mainstream libraries such as D3, Shiny, Bokeh, Leaflet, Lattice. Source: Survey Q22 Which specific data visualization library or tool have you used the most?

Metaphor

The goal is the roof. As with a house, the integrity of it becomes impaired if one column is weak.

Narrative

The narrative here is that non-mainstream visualization libraries are important but to a different degree. Note here that if we had used a pie-chart we would have conveyed a win-lose scarcity narrative, not faithfully representing the win-win ethos of the open-source movement.

THE BRICS FRAMEWORK

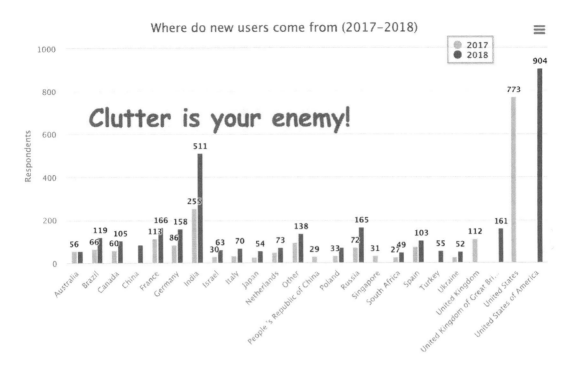

Fig 34 *An example of meaning loss by information overload.*
Source: http://bit.ly/2K7ZLBk

A common way to summarize international data is to count grouping by country. However, this often leads to clutter because there are more than 200 countries in the world. Another common way is to use a geographical world map and to modulate the color of the country with the count. However, some countries are very large in extension while other countries become a pixel on the screen. This is not great for usability.

Exercise: How to summarize 200 countries?

Summarize the previous chart. There are more than 200 countries.

Only 24 are shown in this view[31]. How would you go about this? Draw solutions. Time 5 minutes.

Solution

If we look at the 2018 survey and compare it to the 2017 one, there is an increase of 1145 new respondents that identify as "data scientists". So, where do new data scientist users come from? Fig 34 displays 2018 and 2017 data. However, there are too many countries for a human to make sense of it! Remember that a human brain's working memory is limited to 5-7 chunks [32]. This means we cannot juggle more than seven countries at the same time and neither should your chart. What would Marie Kondo do?

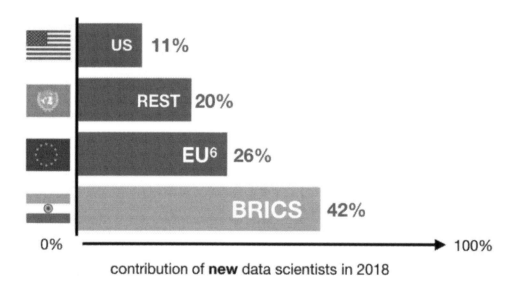

Fig 35 This chart was made with PowerPoint because it was faster than tweaking the parameters of ggplot. Notice how the golden ratio is used across the chart.

Use Mega Regions

One way to summarize more humanely is to group countries in economic megaregions that have a certain degree of homogeneity (cultural or economic). In this case, we apply the BRICS framework. BRICS stands for Brazil, Russia, India, and China. It is a grouping coined by Goldman Sachs to classify countries with similar economic indicators under one label. (The term "BRIC" was coined in 2001 by then-chairman of Goldman Sachs Asset Management, Jim O'Neill).

This framework provides a meaningful way to group countries by bagging them by economic and social development affinity. In this case, we chose four groups: the US, Europe, BRICS, and the rest of the World. When we do that, we see that not only is BRICS the top contributor to growth with 42% of total growth for 2018, but it was also the fastest-growing among the big three. In 2018, in the category "users that define themselves as data scientists", Europe added 302 users, US 131, the rest of the world: 231, and BRICS: 481. By 2020 the growth of BRICS will outnumber Europe and the US combined. Data source: we forked and modified a snippet of the code from Kaggle user ash316 and took the top 20 countries whose respondents identified as "data scientists". EU-6 means the top 6 European countries.

Aesthetics

Note how different font sizes are used in the chart. How the horizontal layout neutralizes the gravity metaphor. And how flags and labels are used. The individual countries' growth added together should stack up to 100%, What narrative would we fall into if the author had used a pie or stack bar?

Narrative

The narrative here is that to be wise, one must look where the ball is going to be not at where it is now. Don't look at absolute numbers of 2018 only, look at growth. Of course, an alternate narrative is that emerging countries are catching up in strategic fields such as data science.

QUIZ: VISUAL SUMMARIES

True or False? Time 5 minutes.

1) Visualizing 200 country names in an 800x1200 display is ridiculous because there are not enough pixels. [True / False]
2) Visualizing 200 countries in a chart violates the 7 chunks limit rule. [T/F]
3) Using PowerPoint or Adobe to build a chart one needs is professional. [T/F]
4) To visualize 'a winner takes all situation' we can use a Marimekko chart. [T/F]
5) House of Shiva is best to visualize all or nothing relations. [T/F]

(Solution on the next page)

Solution

1) Visualizing a chart with 200 country names in an 800x1200 display is ridiculous because there are not enough pixels [True / False]. False. It is ridiculous because a chart with 200 text labels is information overload unusual.

2) Visualizing 200 countries in a chart violates the 7 chunks limit rule [T/F]. True.

3) Using PowerPoint or Adobe to build a chart one needs is professional [T/F]. True.. That is how Bloomberg Businessweek charts are built.

4) To visualize a 'winner takes all' situation we can use a Marimekko chart [T/F]. False. Podium 10x is clearer in this case.

5) House of Shiva is best to visualize 'all or nothing relations' [T/F]. True. If one column is missing the roof falls.

CHAPTER 4

WISDOM   *Visual tools to augment the IQ*

Transform knowledge to wisdom

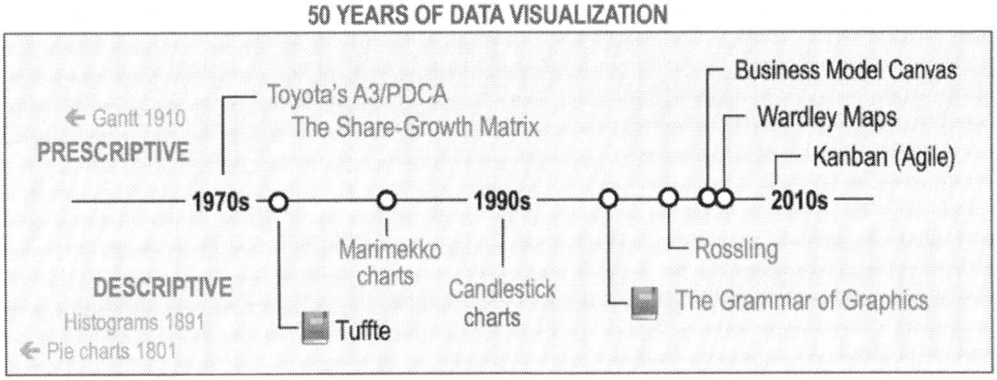

50 YEARS OF DATA VISUALIZATION

Fig 35b *Fifty years of visual Thinking tools. Top: Prescriptive analytics. Bottom: Descriptive analytics.*

So far, we have seen examples of how to transform data into information and information into knowledge. Now let's consider prescriptive analytics — the charts the board room uses to decide what to do in policy and decision making. Unfortunately, policy challenges are complex to deal with. Particularly, when the variables involved have unexpected dependencies that are not properly understood, or even known! A way to deal with these complex problems is to simplify them by describing them more humanely. One popular way is to transform the problem into a map — a process called mapping. Mapping can be done if we just use two dimensions to describe the problem. Once in 2D, the canvas becomes a design space where we can search for solutions. Because we are in a map setting, we can leverage the extraordinary spatial cognitive abilities that have been gifted to us[33].

Glorious examples of "mapping" are war rooms, the BCG growth-share matrix, Gantt charts, The Business Model Canvas, Kanban boards, Gartner's Magic quadrant, and Wardley maps — to date, the most advanced thinking tool to think about strategic innovation.

CASE STUDY: INNOVATION POLICY IN SINGAPORE

Let's start with 2D mapping. Imagine you are a high official in charge of innovation in Singapore. You have only been given Fig 34's data (number of data scientists per country). How would you use this data to inform the next innovation policy looking forward? Hint: A first step is to create situational awareness. One way is to rank the countries, so we can see where we stand. The second step is to use a meaningful indicator in the x-axis. (Solution in the next section).

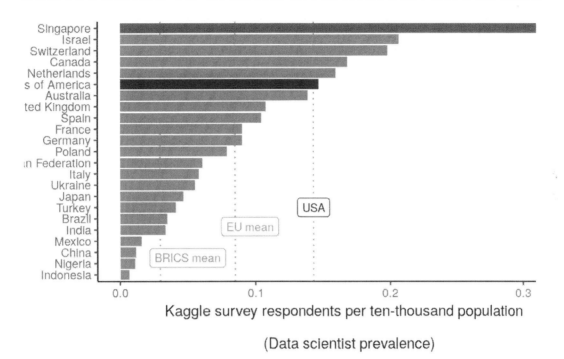

Fig 36 *Two is the maximum amount of colors or grayscales you should use in a chart.*

It's per capita or die

As the economist and comedian, Harald Eia politely implies in his Oslo TEDx Talk, when comparing countries we are hardly ever interested in absolute numbers. In fact, any non-per-capita measure is rather useless. Yet, how often we forget this! Charts not normalized per country population are setting themselves up for stereotypes and unhealthy narratives. From the 2018 Kaggle data science survey, it is possible to count the number of data scientists in each country, and most participants rendered such charts. But how useful is that? We already know that China and the US are large countries, so in absolute numbers, they will also have a larger quantity of data scientists. That is expected.

However, if it is expected it means we already knew it. The more expected, the less information (100% expected means zero information). What is useful, is to look at per capita measures. How do countries compare on data scientist density? In this chart, we highlight Singapore in red and the US (home to the largest survey community, like a center of mass) in black so the reader has a reference point. This chart has a lot going on:

1) USA mean: 0.14 per 10,000
2) EU6 mean*: 0.09 per 10,000
3) BRICS mean*: 0.03 (5x less than the US)

Mind the gap

Mind the gap is a common strategy to think about differences between categories in the data, in this case, countries. Thinking about why the gap exists can help explain the reality that the chart is representing. For example, a linguist might think about the gap in terms of English proficiency and its correlation to the prevalence of data scientists. Is the language barrier an explanatory factor for the gap? What are the policy implications? Note The BRICS, and EU6 mean is the mean of country means, not weighted by respondents. Source: World Bank Population Data 2016, Survey Q11 Current country of residence.

Aesthetics

This color scheme is called the red on grey, it is my favorite scheme for charts. Unlike, other schemes such as purple on grey, it is gender-neutral. However, for it to work, the red surface must be kept to a minimum, otherwise, it comes across as strident.

Narrative

Michael Porter's Competitive Advantage of Nations.

Exercise

Let's take Fig 36 chart a step further. Earlier we saw that frameworks can help the reader make sense of new information. Using the *global innovation index*, how would you relate it to the prevalence of data scientists? Use 2D mapping. Time 5 minutes. (Solution in the next section).

HOW TO USE SCATTER PLOTS AS A CANVAS?

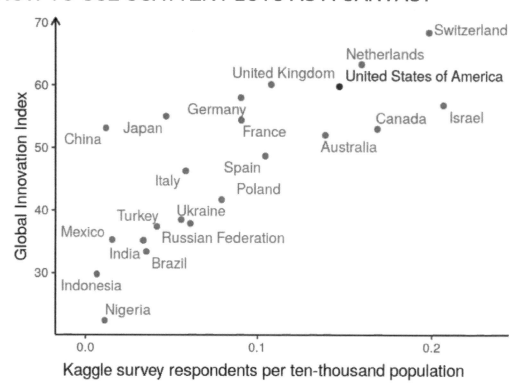

Fig 37 *A scatter plot between two correlated variables always yields a similar cloud.*

As Mr. Wardley would say — When you need to understand the territory it helps to have a map. Here we use 2D mapping by scattering the countries along two dimensions. The technique of projecting into two dimensions has been successfully used in famous charts such as Wardley Maps, the BCG growth-share matrix, The Urgent-Important matrix, and Gartner's magic quadrant. This map can be used to cluster countries by policy to help elucidate success factors that influence the position in the map (See also Hans Rosling's Gapminder).

Narrative

Porter's Competitive Advantage of Nations.

About the Innovation Index

Every year, INSEAD MBA, Cornel University, and the WIPO publish the Global Innovation Index. In 2018, the most innovative country was Switzerland. A Spearman rank correlation between GII and user prevalence yields 79%.

Exercise

Let's take this chart a step further. One of the most valuable skills is prediction. Given Fig 37, can you predict where Japan will be 10 years from now? Use a linear regression. Time 5 minutes. (Solution in the next section).

FORECASTING WITH MEAN-REVERSION

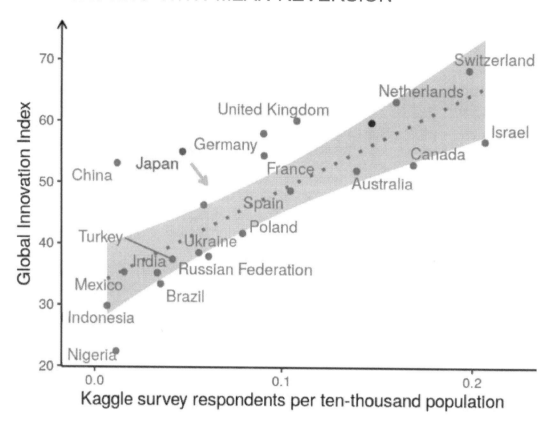

Fig 38 *Mean reversion, always right in the long run?*

Here, we just added a regression line and removed the outlier Singapore. The 95% standard error margin is shown in grey. Some countries are below and some above. Highlighted, (next to the arrow), is Japan, as an outlier with high in Global Innovation Index (y-axis), but low in x-axis relative to peers. Let's assume that the principle of **mean reversion** applies here as a baseline predictor and a "hidden hand" continually pushes countries towards the mean (dotted line). The principle of mean reversion is based on the idea that there are no permanent competitive advantages. (See introduction chapter in Blue Ocean Strategy book) or nations. It has shown its worth, particularly in finance. For example, in betting on the composition of the DOW JONES, very few companies have what it takes to last long in the Dow Jones. Of the original members of the index formed in 1896, only GE remains.

Reflection

What can we forecast about the 2019 GII rank position of Japan? Applying the principle of mean reversion, it is unlikely that Japan will increase its rank because it is already high. Even if Japan catches up in data scientist prevalence, likely, it will still go down (towards the mean with inertia). Indexes are just weights. Assuming the Data Science weight in the innovation economy will only increase in the coming decades and that the GII index calculation method will be updated accordingly, what countries are more likely to improve their "nominal" ranking in 2019? When the GII index weights are rebalanced, how likely is it that countries such as Canada, Australia will jump a few places? Source: Global Innovation Index 2018, World Bank Population Data 2016, Question 11 - Current country of residence.

A note on the origin of linear regression

The name linear regression as in the line that minimizes the sum of the square of the errors was popularized in a paper where the principle of "regression to the mean" was verified in how offspring height is related to the parent's height. Spoiler alert! Only 60% of the offspring's height is explained by the parents' heights. The rest is explained by the mean of the race. This means that the Mean reversion principle applies in height with a 40% influence approximately. However, the mathematical method is completely unrelated to any concept of regression. The paper got famous and the regression word stuck to the method. A great trick question is to ask students to explain why linear regression is called linear regression. I am always amazed at the inventiveness of some students[34].

HOW TO USE 2D MAPS FOR BUSINESS STRATEGY?

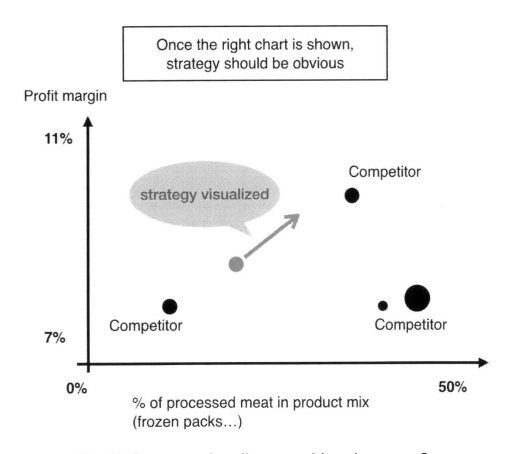

Fig 39 *Can you visualize a problem in a map?*

Reframe it

One of the most important roles of a data scientist is to realize what the customer needs when the customer cannot articulate his own needs (see the *Jobs-to-be-done* theory). This skill is what distinguishes the A+ data scientist from the rest. The chart here is adapted from the book *The Accidental Investment Banker*. The author, a banker, came up with it during a business engagement. He used it to map out the M&A strategy for a client. Once he made this chart, everybody in the room could visualize the strategy. In his book, he credits this chart as an important moment in his career as clients were amazed by it.

THE GAP MATRIX

How Digitally Advanced Is Your Sector?

An analysis of digital assets, usage, and labor.

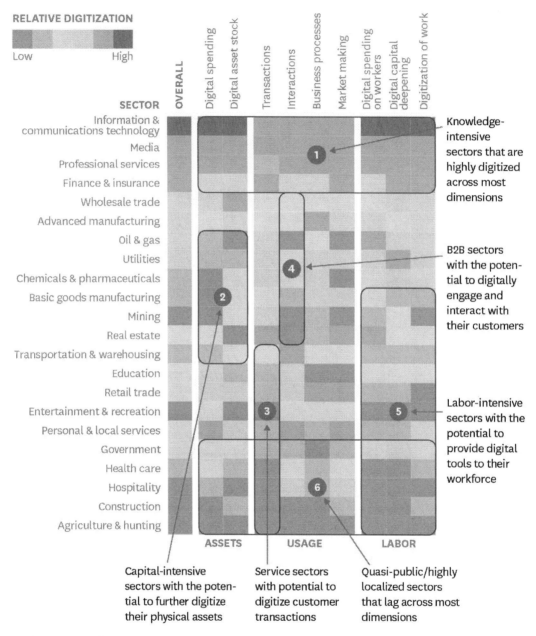

RELATIVE DIGITIZATION

Low — High

SECTOR — OVERALL — Digital spending — Digital asset stock — Transactions — Interactions — Business processes — Market making — Digital spending on workers — Digital capital deepening — Digitization of work

ASSETS — USAGE — LABOR

Sectors:
Information & communications technology
Media
Professional services
Finance & insurance
Wholesale trade
Advanced manufacturing
Oil & gas
Utilities
Chemicals & pharmaceuticals
Basic goods manufacturing
Mining
Real estate
Transportation & warehousing
Education
Retail trade
Entertainment & recreation
Personal & local services
Government
Health care
Hospitality
Construction
Agriculture & hunting

1 — Knowledge-intensive sectors that are highly digitized across most dimensions

4 — B2B sectors with the potential to digitally engage and interact with their customers

5 — Labor-intensive sectors with the potential to provide digital tools to their workforce

2 — Capital-intensive sectors with the potential to further digitize their physical assets

3 — Service sectors with potential to digitize customer transactions

6 — Quasi-public/highly localized sectors that lag across most dimensions

SOURCE DATA ANALYSIS AND EXPERT INTERVIEWS CONDUCTED BY THE MCKINSEY GLOBAL INSTITUTE — © HBR.ORG

Fig 40a Business Innovation is sometimes as easy as finding a white space. Source: McKinsey Global Institute[35]

Finding gaps in the market

Another use of 2D design space is to find overlooked or underserved segments. Also known as "**gaps**". We can apply this method to matrixes too. Examples are a company-employee skills matrix, technology roadmaps, and the innovation matrix. In Fig 40, McKinsey took a sectorial view. However, other viewpoints can yield discoveries too. For example: instead of viewing by sector we could view by the software vendor (Salesforce, JIRA, Autodesk…).

The Periodic table

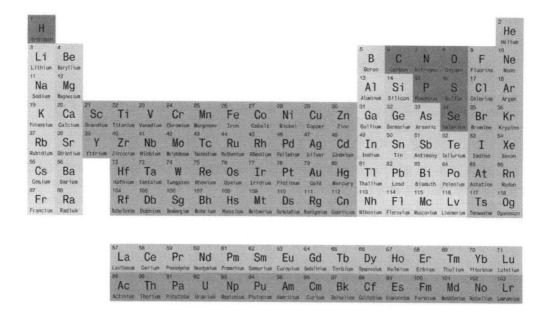

Fig 40*b The most useful visualization in the history of Science?*
Source: Bloomberg BusinessWeek, 2019.

A famous application of the Gap Matrix is Mendeleev's 1869 Periodic Table of Elements. In 1869, 150 years ago, Dmitri Mendeleev published a periodic table of the chemical elements is based on properties that appeared with some regularity as he laid out the elements from lightest to heaviest. When Mendeleev proposed his periodic table, he noted gaps. At the time, only 63 of the 118 known elements identified today were known. Then he predicted the properties of five undiscovered elements -- a genius coup for any young scientist[36]. Mendeleev's visual predictions spurred a discovery race. Shockingly, he never received the Nobel prize – a testament to scientific rivalries, but also of how visual thinking has been historically despised by an academia that is often dominated by word-oriented thinking.

THE INNOVATION MATRIX

"The Innovation Matrix is a knowledge discovery tool" –
Leo Tschirsky

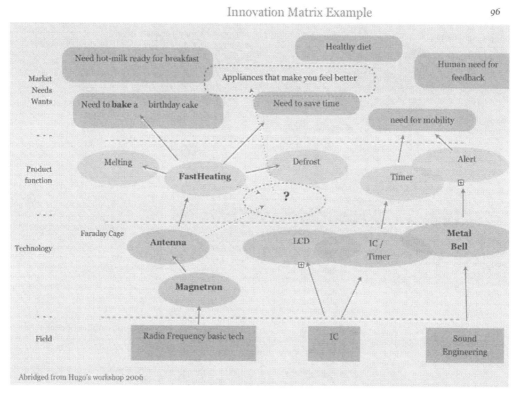

Fig 41 *The Innovation Matrix (IM)*[37].

Leo Tschirsky, Professor Emeritus of Business Management at the Swiss Federal Institute of Technology (ETH), facilitated this microwave oven workshop in Tokyo Institute of Technology around 2006. I was lucky to be there. The **IM** helps to formalize and organize functional relations between:

1) Market needs
2) Product functions

3) Technology
4) Science fields

How to use

1. Draw a matrix format by rows
   Write the market needs (Why people buy ovens)

   Product functions (heat, boil...)

   Technologies behind those functions (Magnetron, LCD...)

   Basic science field supporting those technologies. (RF, IC)

2. Link concepts with arrows
   Clarify

   Seek deep truths

   Use 5-Why root cause analysis, jobs-to-be-done theory

   Once your product is clear and mapped out...

3. Innovate

Now that you have a clear picture of relationships between value, customer needs, costs, and technology. You are in a better position to innovate using a variety of techniques such as:

1) Brainstorming
2) Planning an ideo style shopping cart workshop
3) Using Edward de Bono creativity tools
4) Finding gaps
5) Serving new needs with exiting functions

Exercise

Groups of four. Time 20 minutes. Think about this microwave and its components…

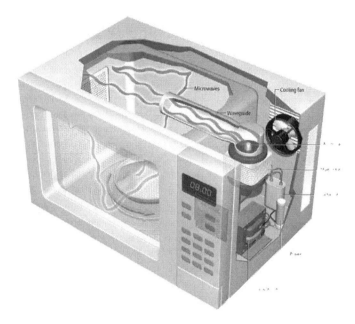

Fig 42 *The cyclotron is the element that generates the microwaves.*

You have been hired by a microwave oven brand. Recently, due to Chinese competition, the oven margins are paper thin so the survival of the company might very well depend on you coming up with a new oven design for which customers want to pay more. **Required**. Use the IM to innovate the microwave.

Solution

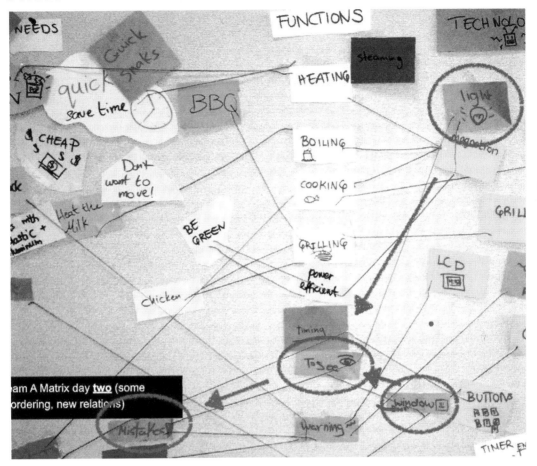

Fig 43-44 *Functional Innovation example, can we replace light and window with a cheaper component with the same function?*

Light and oven window seem two unrelated technologies in an oven. However, they serve a common need: The need to check for mistakes! ***Cost of (Window +Light) > Cost of (X)?*** Consider the cost of a window + light. Their sole purpose is now clear. Can X do their function better, cheaper? Let's find X!

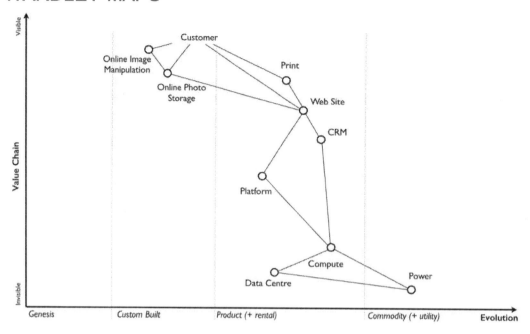

Fig 45 *A Wardley map, Simon Wardley* CC BY-SA 4.0 .

A Wardley map can be thought of as a 2D mapping of commoditization trend vs value chain of a product. Alternatively, it can also be viewed as an evolution of Leo Tschirsky's Innovation Matrix. In any case, when there are dilemmas about whether to outsource or not, this is the go-to tool in 2019. So far we have seen a few visualization tools used in business and policymaking. However, visualization is also used in coaching. Let's see an example called the wheel of life from 1960.

WHEEL OF LIFE

"A chart to think about your life goals"

Amy is a working, single mom who just resigned from a Fortune 500 job. A successful career woman in her own right, Amy just left her ascending executive role because she wanted to travel less and spend more quality time with her 14-year-old teenage daughter. I am sitting with Amy. We are meeting to talk about life, career, and charts, yes charts! Amy is about to show me a chart I have never seen before. She calls it the **Wheel of Life**. This chart, she tells me, was instrumental in helping her realize that she needed to change her life.

How to use

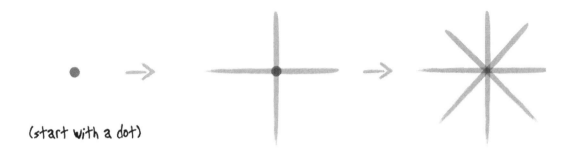

(start with a dot)

Fig 46 *Start with a dot in the middle of a paper.*

First, you draw spokes. Eight spokes of a wheel. Each spoke represents a different category of your life and will help you measure your satisfaction in each area of your life. The first one is Money (How satisfied are you with the money you have saved/make?) Second, Career (How satisfied are you with your path, progress, and current career?). Third, Wellness (both spiritual/mental and physical). Then, Friends & Family, Love, Fun, Physical Environment (Do you like the country, city/ house/ neighborhood you are in?), and finally, spiritual and personal growth. We put a grade on each category marking a dot on the spoke on a scale of 1 to 10, 1 being at the center and 10 being away from the center, and then we connect the dots.

Connecting the dots

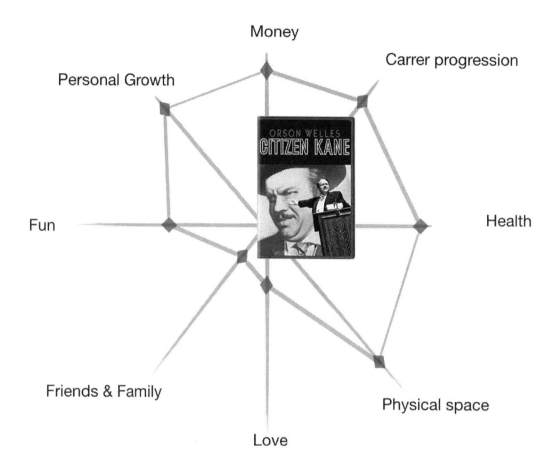

Fig 47 *Citizen Kane-type wheel of Life.*

As I connect the dots of my chart, a chill goes up my spine. My wheel of life is not round! It looks like an asteroid and has a big dip where the spoke of love is. Is that bad? "Oh, well," I think, mortified, I guess I need to reprioritize my life.

An x-ray of your life

Then Amy leans over and says, "This is the snapshot of your life. I learned this exercise at a drop-in class at Stanford. It turned out to be one of the most useful things I learned there because it helped me visualize my **blind spots**. Many of my classmates did this chart too, and they were just as shocked as you are now..." Then she adds, "The typical comment of my classmate was: Here I am, focusing on my career and personal development, as I have done all my life, while equally or more important parts of my life are being neglected." The wheel of life, together with other visualization tools such as *the good time journal,* is part of the **design your life** trend where design principles of iteration, visualization, and design thinking, in general, are applied to coaching. The results are spectacular. To learn more, the book by Atari co-founder *Designing your life* is a great start.

Exercise: Wheel of Life

Make your own Wheel of Life. Look at it. Now, How would you make it more compelling than Fig 47? Time 7 minutes. (Solution on the next page)

Solution

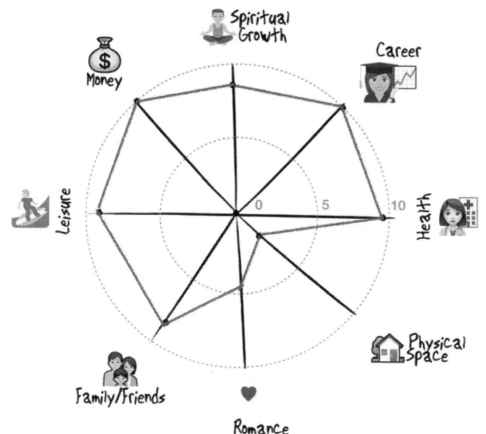

Fig 48 *Icons, use to reduce the time to understand a chart.*

Icons and emoji are an underused resource in chart making. On the other hand, emoji use is correlated with employee engagement

INTERACTIVE EXPLORATION

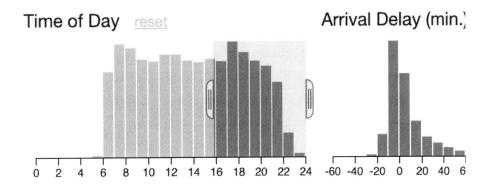

Time of Day reset   Arrival Delay (min.)

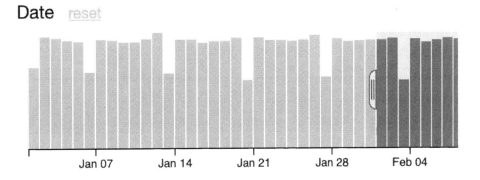

Date reset

February 09, 2001

11:56 PM	LAS	LAX
11:50 PM	MCI	MDW
11:45 PM	PHX	SAN

Fig 49 *A screenshot of a real-time, visual SQL inner join operation between three tables; Source: Square 2001.*

Square's Crossfilter

Crossfilter is a JavaScript library for exploring large multivariate datasets in the browser. Extremely fast (<30ms), it allows "Doherty threshold" interaction with coordinated views, even with datasets containing a million or more records; Square Inc. built it in 2001 to power analytics for Square Register.

Exercise

Groups of two. Time 12 minutes. Using Square's Crossfilter demo, find three insights about air travel. Example: To avoid delays fly in the morning. Visualize your findings.

QUIZ: SUPPORTING DECISIONS

True or False? Time 10 minutes.

1) Working with per capita measures is the only rational way to compare countries. [True / False]
2) The principle of mean reversion states that, in the long run, a 'hidden hand' pushes outliers towards the mean. [T/F]
3) The gap matrix is used primarily to discover niche or gaps in the market. [T/F]
4) Wardley maps have rendered the Innovation Matrix obsolete. [T/F]
5) The Crossfilter library is an appropriate choice to visualize linear relationships between two variables such as delays and departure time. [T/F]

Solution

1) Working with per capita measures is the only rational way to compare countries. [True / False]. True.

2) The principle of mean reversion states that, in the long run, a 'hidden hand' pushes outliers towards the mean [T/F]. True. There are no long-lasting competitive advantages [98].

3) The gap matrix is used primarily to discover niche or gaps in the market [T/F]. True. However, it can also be used in other areas.

4) Wardley maps have rendered Innovation Matrix obsolete [T/F]. False. Innovation Matrix is still better than Wardley to do product innovation and to map a product to its market.

5) The Crossfilter library is an appropriate choice to visualize linear relationships between two variables such as delays and departure time [T/F]. False. A scatter plot is clearer. Crossfilter is great for EDA.

Fig 50 *Jazz hands, use to make a visual compelling.*

In this chapter, we will see hacking strategies to make your chart memorable. Now that you know the principles of meaningful chart making (by reducing information overload, linking to frameworks, fitting narratives, and leveraging visual metaphors), let's look at simple tips on how to jazz it up, or in design thinking jargon, make it "pop". Pop means it pops into the eyes. My favorite resources on this are: Dan Roam's books, Information is Beautiful by McCandless, and the Instagram account "chartr". Be careful! Some charts are so beautiful on their own that they are like a piece of art in their own right. In any case, remember, the chart should never be the main character of your story, what matters is the narrative (message) and how well it is communicated to your audience.

Unfortunately, aesthetically pleasing visuals and a visual that gets the job done do not always coincide. Incidentally, this is one of the reasons that in an Advertising agency you will see the art director and account manager always at odds, the art director wants to win ad awards to go to Cannes Lions Creativity Festival, the manager wants effective advertisement. Let's see the main techniques used to make a chart "pop".

USE ARROWS TO UNBOUND YOUR THINKING

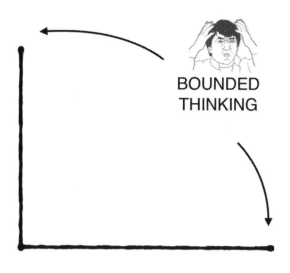

BOUNDED
THINKING

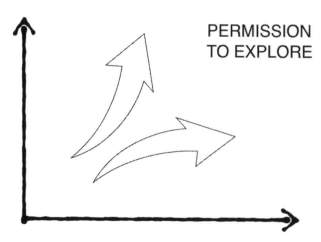

PERMISSION
TO EXPLORE

*Fig 51 The arrows give you **permission** to think beyond.*

HOW TO DECLUTTER A BAR CHART

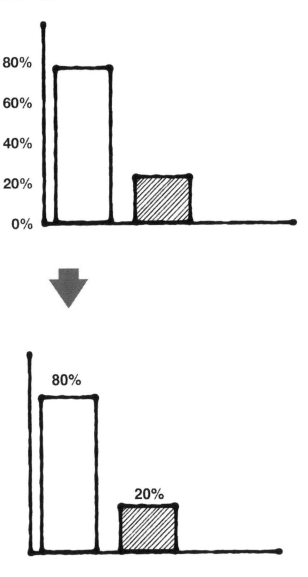

Fig 52 *Marie Kondo applies the principle of throwing away things in one's life that do not spark joy.*

HOW TO DECLUTTER A PIE CHART

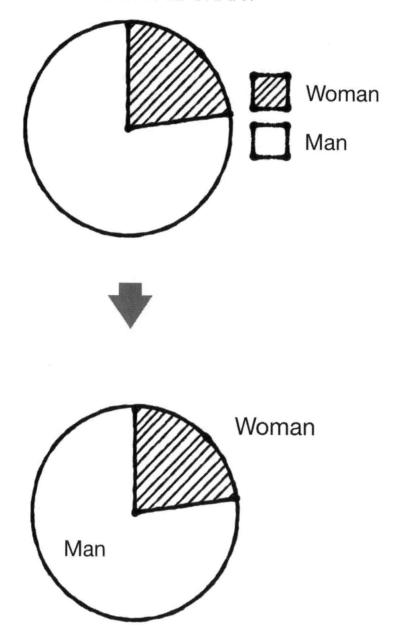

Fig 53 *Animation on decluttering a pie chart bit.ly/2OgCLUO*

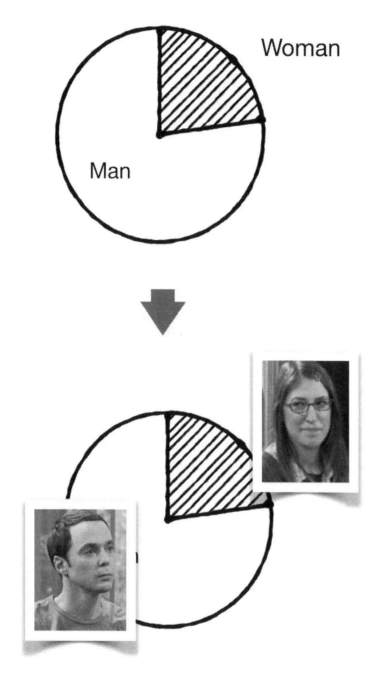

Fig 54 Humans are adept at recognizing faces.

Did you know that we can recognize a face faster than many other objects in the world? Use it! In 2007 Honda used this principle when they designed a motorbike that, from the back, looked like a human face (anthropomorphic).

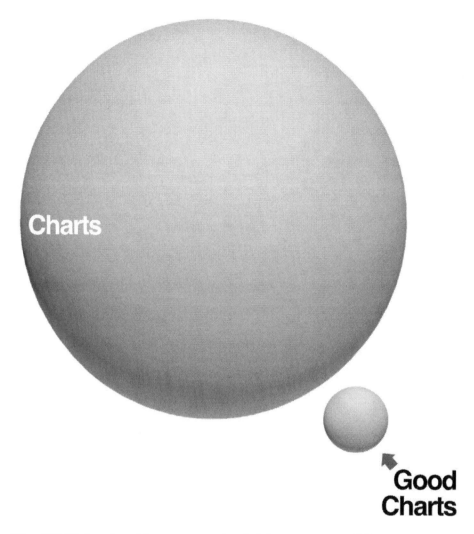

Fig 55 *This chart has an astonishing range of four orders of magnitude.*

How to calculate the dynamic range in a planet chart. In a planet chart, the dynamic range is n^3, where n is the times the small planet radius fits into the big one. In Fig 56, n=12. Therefore, $n^3 = 12^3 =$ 1720. Therefore, the share of the small planet is approximately 1 in (1720+1), 0.05%.

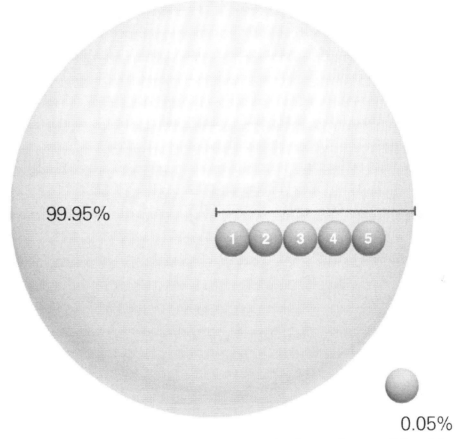

Fig 56 *The small planet fits 1720 times in the volume of the big one.*

Other successful attempts to visualize enormous differences are the famous post "What does a Ph.D. mean to you", and the 1977 film Powers of Ten; both used the 2D zoom technique to illustrate gargantuan size contrasts. However, of all chart metaphors, the planet metaphor is excellent to visualize vast differences. See the next page to find out why.

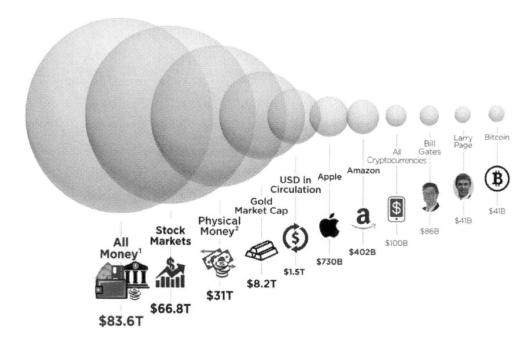

Fig 57 *Humans are evolutionarily adapted to estimate mass from height.*

The dynamic range of this chart is an astonishing **four orders** of magnitude! It can visualize 41bn and something 20,000 times larger. This chart was combined with the Fear Of Missing Out (FOMO) narrative before the Bitcoin crash of January 2018. Original source: HowMuch.net.

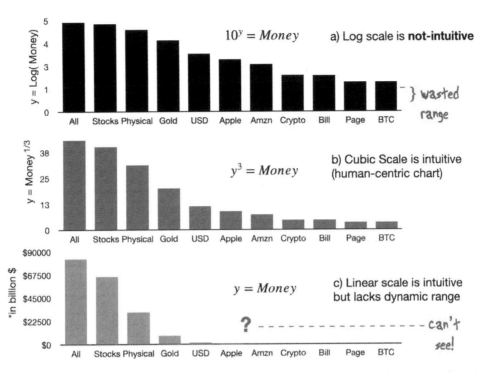

Fig 58 *Comparison between a) Log of value, b) Cubic root of value (Radius of equivalent weight sphere), and c) Linear scale.*

In Fig 58, note how (a) has the most dynamic range but is not intuitive; (b) is the radius of the sphere equivalent. It would be intuitive if expressed as volume, like in Fig 57; (c) is a linear scale; is intuitive, but lacks dynamic range.

Why 3D spheres work so well

We, humans, have evolved to estimate the weight of an animal from sight. Of course, this was a very useful skill for our ancestors in the Savannah. Notice how much easier it is to understand relative sizes when we use volume, versus any other option. For primates, estimating the weight of a fellow primate visually was a crucial survival skill useful to determine how dangerous the threat of an opponent was before contact. Given that most living forms have a

116

similar weight density, a way to do this was by estimating volume. At the same time, we humans struggle to understand bar charts when the bars differ more than 2 orders of magnitude. Luckily, if shown 2D projections of 3D objects, most humans can estimate the weight well. This comes in handy to compare magnitudes as different as 3 or 4 orders of magnitude on a flat surface such as this book. Using the cubic relation, a 1 to 10 change in height becomes a 1 to 1,000 change in weight — a great dynamic range.

Log charts

Note that the log plot solves the issue of dynamic range but we humans are not born with *logarithmic* intuition built-in (Fig 58). In other words, a kid will understand the balls, but it takes hours for undergrads to become familiar with semi-log plots.

HOW MANY SOLAR PANELS
ARE NEEDED TO POWER THE USA?

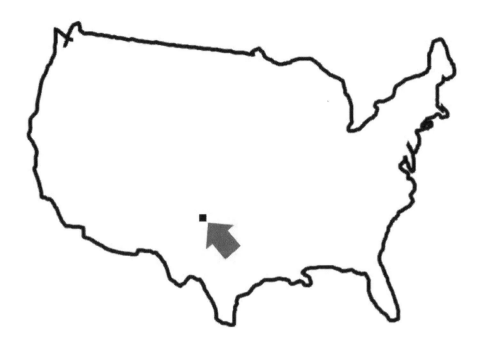

Fig 59 *In 2017, Elon Musk used such a chart template to advocate for Solar Energy. — It was a flop.*

Fig 59 narrative is scarcity. In 2017, Elon Musk used a chart like this one. He was advocating for Solar Energy. He said, "We just need one pixel of the map covered in panels to power the whole USA, remember just one pixel." It was a flop. Why? Because it connected to a win-lose narrative. It is also hard to trust what we cannot see (one pixel is not a great visualization). Unfortunately, 2D charts do not have enough dynamic range to visualize differences larger than 2 orders of magnitude. He was trying to visualize 4 orders.

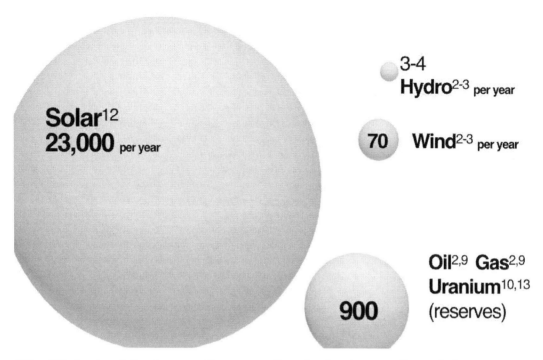

Solar[12]
23,000 per year

3-4
Hydro[2-3] per year

70 **Wind**[2-3] per year

Oil[2,9] **Gas**[2,9]
Uranium[10,13]
(reserves)

900

Fig 60 *A chart that uses the growth mindset narrative. Adapted from Q-Cells.*

Fig 60 narrative is the ***growth mindset.*** It visualizes more than 5 orders effortlessly. Circa the year 2005, German solar maker Q-cells used a similar chart in their PR. This chart is more effective and trusted than Fig 59 because it connects us to the growth mindset narrative by visualizing the astonishing abundance of **renewable** energy available.

STORYTELLING AGE-BIAS WITH HUMOR

Fig 61 is based on an arrest dataset provided by the Minneapolis Police department and other sources. It was published in 2018. It shows the correlation between arrests with no charges and the age difference between policeman and subject.

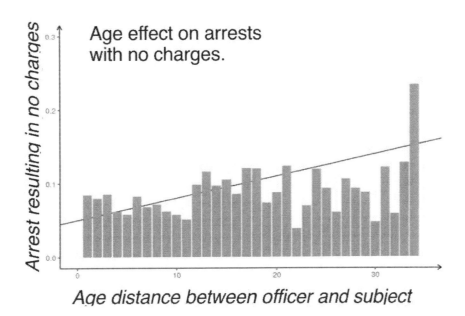

Fig 61 *Of all the biases, age is one of the most pervasive and less talked about.*

Dataset source: http://bit.ly/2JXWP9d. Regression is shown in blue. If one considers not being charged as a positive outcome, then one would prefer interacting with an older policeman, but if one considers "a no charge arrest" as a negative outcome, then one would prefer interacting with a cop closer to one's age. The lower the age gap, the lower the chance of not being charged.

Exercise

Make Fig 61 chart more compelling. Time 3 minutes.

Solution

Fig 62 *Use personas to make a chart memorable.*

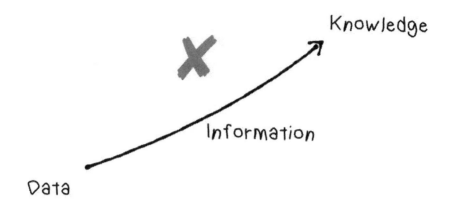

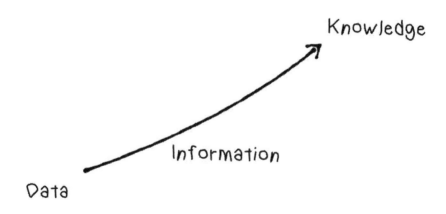

Fig 63 *Which one feels more harmonious?*

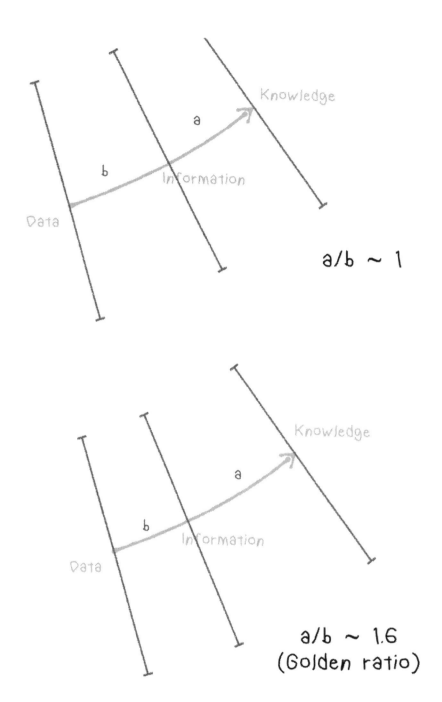

$a/b \sim 1$

$a/b \sim 1.6$
(Golden ratio)

Fig 64 *Never miss a chance to use the golden ratio.*

Did you know that if you show two different cards to a human, she will choose the one whose proportions are the closest to the 1.6?

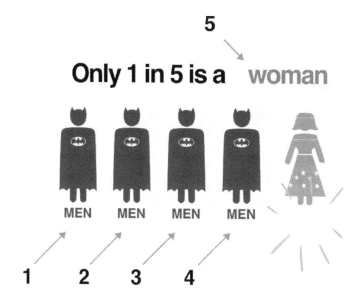

Fig 65 *Use twists to make your chart stick.*

In *improvisation*[38] theatre, we always say that a good story should have a *twist*. An effective twist is what makes a TikTok video viral, or in business cases, the so-called Aha! moment. We can use negative space to create twists in charts. In this case, the reader expects to find label #5 in a certain place but it is not there! This sends the brain into search mode[39]. When a few milliseconds later the brain finds the missing label, some endorphins are released. A bonus of this twist is that it fail-proofs (Poka-Yoke[40]) the chart — changing the label location makes sure that the reader will not miss the title. Now that we know the main hacks to make a chart pop, let's see a few examples.

CASE STUDY: SWEDISH ICE-CREAM CONSUMPTION

Evaluate the following chart. Then prose a better way to visualize it.
Required: 300 words essay + two mockup sketches of proposed
improved visualization. Time 25 minutes.

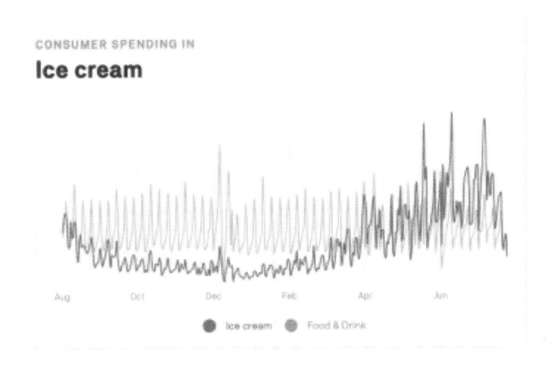

Fig 66 *Sales of ice cream in Sweden, Iceland, and Finland. Source:
Meniga/Wrapp.*

Solution

Main observations

1) This chart contains useful information such as weekend sales are higher than Wednesday sales, and Summer sales are higher than Winter. However, the chart timeline is not optimal to showcase this.

2) To give this chart more utility, connect it to other knowledge. For example, comparing to sales in Spain, (where the Winter: Summer ratio of sales is lower, 4x vs 10x in Sweden).

3) This chart lacks narrative. An example of a narrative could be how culture influences consumer habits. Example: "It's funny actually what happens in Sweden during summer months, we sort of lose our minds. We eat, drink and swim like we never saw the sun - that's what happens when you live close to the North Pole and July comes.". Thérèse Lundquist -- Head of Marketing & PR at Wrapp.

Color choices

4) Orange: cute at first glance, annoying after 20 seconds.

Timeline

5) The data is weekly and yearly periodical, therefore a yearly or weekly periodical time scale would reduce clutter. For example, a weekly radar chart.

Alternative charts

6) Radar weekly.
7) Bar plot monthly, weekly with iso-measures of ice cream.
8) The grey line is constant therefore carries no meaning (remove?).

Other **suggestions**

9) Normalize per capita & by number of users.
10) Annotate Christmas weekend and other peak days
11) Explode into a scatter between temperature (x-axis), sales (y-axis). The color of a dot represents the day of the week.
12) Calculate % of sales due to temperature and % sales due to seasonality from a linear regression analysis using as factors summer and weekends.
13) Use Crossfilter to let users explore and discover hidden relationships for the variables weekday, month, temperature, sales of ice cream, and individual variance in consumption.

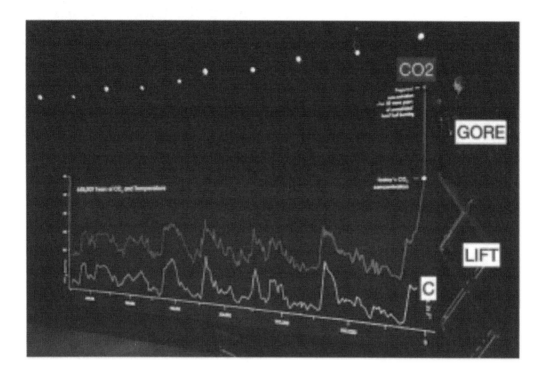

Fig 67 *Al Gore's CO₂ Emissions Chart was not viral.*

In 2006 Al Gore's presented this CO_2 Emissions Chart. X-axis span is +100 years; In Y-axis, the red line is the concentration of CO_2; the blue line is temperature. Note the high correlation between both. To the right is Al Gore on top of a scissor lift. It was a flop. How would you help Al Gore visualize global warming? Time 25 minutes.

Solution

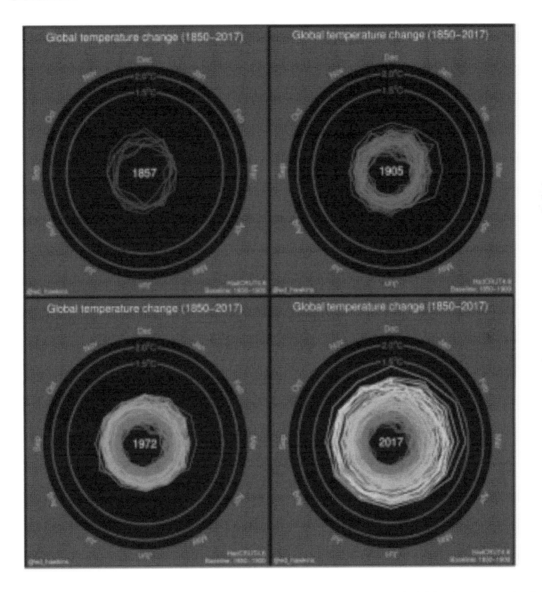

Fig 68 *Ed Hawkins made this **spiral chart** in May 2016. It went viral in minutes.*

From <u>Pies vs. Bars</u>, we know that humans are **more** sensitive to circular than linear change. If we want the chart to align with the narrative that "climate change is an emergency", then let's leverage that!

Fig 69 *Most wanted Data Science skills in 2019. Source* <u>KDnuggets</u>. *Image at original resolution. (Might appear blurry on some devices).*

In 2019, Gregory Piatetsky, editor of *KDnuggets*, published this chart. It used three visualization principles:

- **Color** labeling to identify the cold/hot skills. Red for hot skills, blue for core/cold skills

- **Dot** size to indicate a magnitude, and

- **Mapping** to a 2D space (but did not utilize its design potential)

The chart was based on a poll. The poll had just two questions: Which skills/knowledge areas do you currently **have**? And Which skills do you **want** to add or improve? KDnuggets received 1,500 answers, and the aggregates by skill look as follows.

Table 1. Aggregates of the survey.

Skill	Have it	Want it	ratio
Python	71.2%	37.1%	0.52
Data Visualization	69.0%	**25.3%**	0.37
Critical Thinking	66.7%	15.5%	0.23
Excel	66.5%	4.6%	0.07
Source: KDnuggets			

How might we visualize this data in a more meaningful way? What design space is most appropriate given the data? Time 4 hours. Hint: See Magic Quadrants.

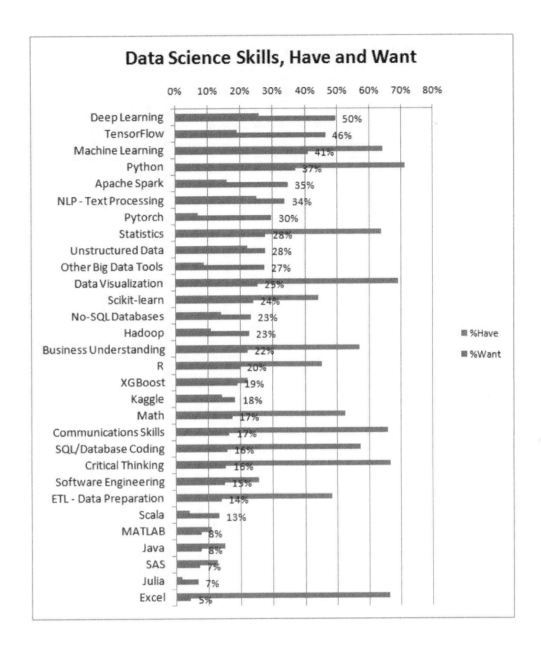

Fig 69b *Fig from Most wanted Data Science skills in 2019. Source KDnuggets. Image at original resolution (might appear blurry on some devices).*

Solution

Let's apply what we have learned so far. (Find a why, transform data into information, synthesize knowledge by linking to frameworks, make it useful for decision making). Before finding a why let's first explore the data.

Step 1 Summarize the data into information

The first instinct is to do a scatter plot to identify interesting clusters. The x-axis can be the percentage of respondents that have a given skill, and the y-axis, percentage of respondents that would like to have that skill (want). However, there are too many data points for a human to make sense of it. It is a textbook case of death by information overload and in Fig 70 we used the Jackie Chan meme to convey it.

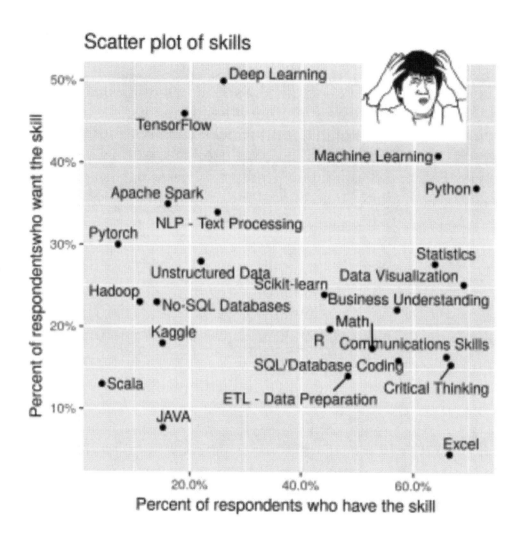

Fig 70 *A victim of information overload?*

Step 2 Apply four clusters to create meaning

How to transform this information into knowledge? Let's take a cue from the **Gartner magic quadrant**, a framework used in IT business intelligence. It reduces complexity to human levels by using a quadrant hierarchy (Fig 71).

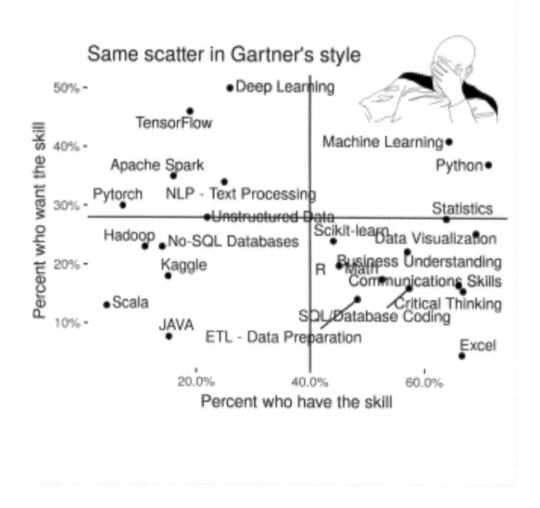

Fig 71 *Gartner uses the quadrants framework to cluster, reduce complexity and make meaning.*

Step 3 Align the axes with the arrow of value

However, Fig 71 is far from ready. The y-axis is aligned with the gravity metaphor (highly wanted, high y). However, the x-axis is not aligned with another unspoken rule, (this one by Guy Kawasaki): "you want (desired goals) to be high and to the right". In this case, the most desired skill (Deep Learning) is on the wrong side – we need to flip the x-axis, (Fig 72).

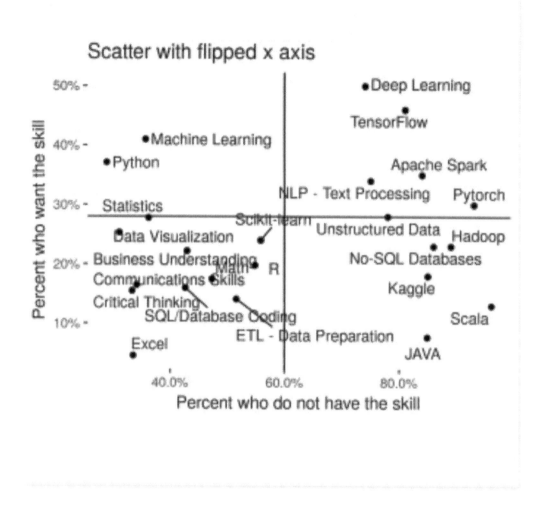

Fig 72 *Goals should be "high and to the right" – Guy Kawasaki.*

Step 4 Apply Ad principles, make it memorable

If we make a chart and no one remembers it. Did it still happen? In Fig 72, we grouped the skills into four categories but what good are they if no one remembers them? One way to help your audience to remember is personas (memes in Gen-Z speak). Let's apply user personas. In Fig 73 each quadrant means:

1) **Unwanted skills** (Have but, don't want = Excel)
2) **No-thank-you skills** (don't want and don't have = JAVA)
3) **Hot skills** (want but don't have = Tensor Flow)
4) **Loved skills** (want and have = Python)

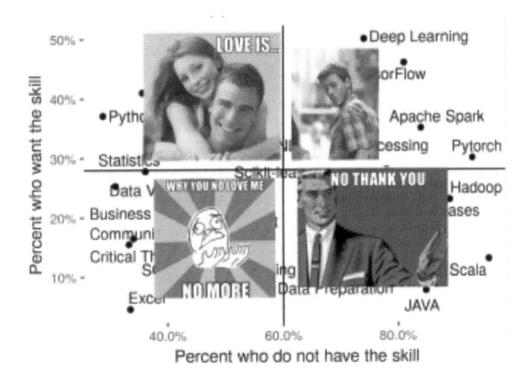

Fig 73 *Pop culture, use to make your chart stick.*

144

Step 5 Organize the information with labels, stratification and hierarchies (Information architecture)

Don't be afraid to red pen your canvas! Captions are an opportunity to clarify meaning and add punch to your story (not everyone is visual). Note how in Fig 74 we broke the symmetry by tilting the "loved" label, that is Feng-Shui for charts. We also added a twist in the Java quadrant by not having a label for it. This ensures that the reader will go to this quadrant after visiting all the others. The label for this quadrant is inside the meme (No thank you).

Note how we have layered information in hierarchies (meme, quadrant labels, quadrant representative). We have respected the seven-chunk limit in each layer to avoid overload. Meaning was achieved by linking to an existing framework and organizing the data into quadrants. Then adding labels.

Step 6 Be aware and clarify the narrative

Finally, charts should have a purpose. It is reasonable to go through the process of knowledge creation without knowing why. Once knowledge has been found and visualized, the why will be easy to find. My personal why for this chart is: "I like to see more Python and less Java in my classroom".

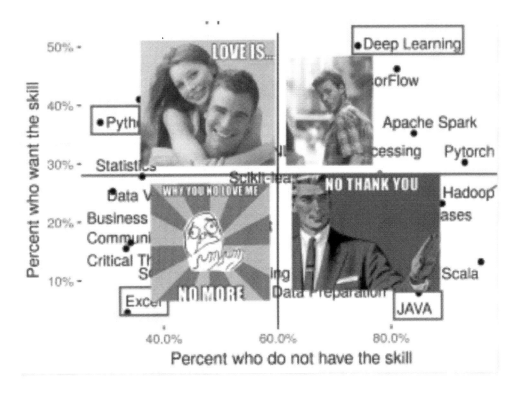

Fig 74 *Can Magic Quadrants make a scatter plot memorable?*

Step 7 Connect to another reference framework to create more knowledge

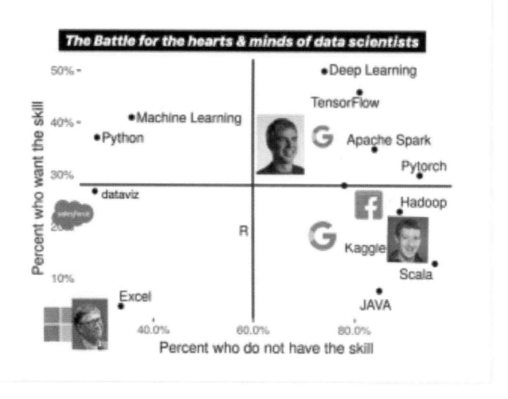

Fig 75 *Salesforce acquired Tableau. Why?*

Now that we created knowledge, can we use this chart as a thinking tool? One way is to imagine contexts where this chart might be useful. Where could this chart be used to create situational awareness? The figurative "cloud wars" between Microsoft and Google are fought via proxies such PowerBI, Kaggle, and other cloud software lock-in levers. A similar playbook developed in the '90s in the database market. Fig 75 visualizes who sponsors which language to see where allegiances stand.

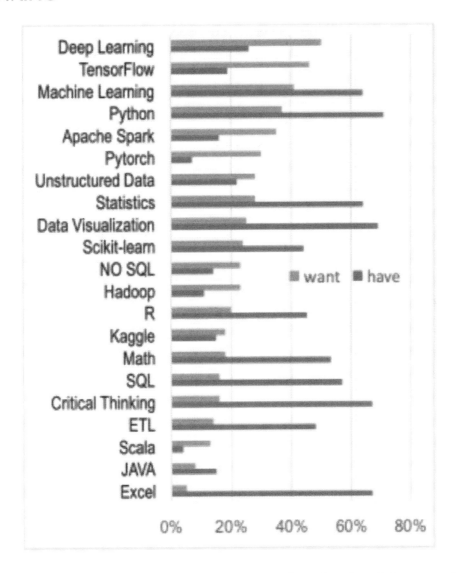

Fig 76 Data science skills - *How to conjugate absolute magnitude and relative differences. Source: KDnuggets. Image at original resolution (might appear blurry in some devices)*

In the same post, KDnuggets posted this chart. The purpose of this chart was to display the **gap** between *have* and *wanted skills* while not losing perspective of the absolute magnitudes involved in each skill. Why does this chart fail? How would you declutter this chart and make it more meaningful <u>without loss of information</u>? (no summarization). Time 1 hour. Hint: See waterfall stack bars with negative components by McKinsey.

Solution

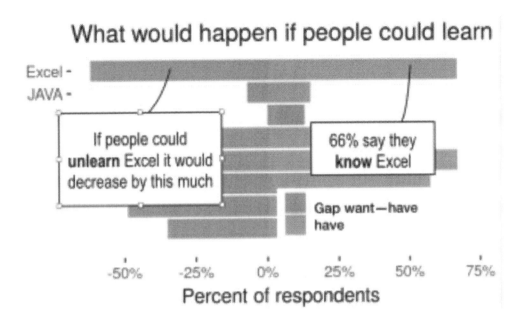

Fig 77 *If people could unlearn things, would they? (Only 3 items are shown due to resolution limits of the device)*

Step 1 Define the differential (gap)

The author wants to display for each skill three attributes:

1) **Have** skills
2) **Wanted** skills
3) Wanted minus have (the gap)

Of these three only two are independent variables. Applying the principle of eliminating superfluous information we display only two. Have (as the underlying) and the gap (want minus the underlying).

Step 2 Predict applying hypotheses

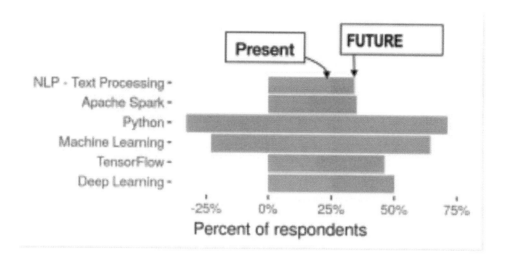

Fig 78 *What if you could learn anything you wanted? (Only 6 items are shown due to resolution limits of the device)*

Step 3 Evolve your narrative

This chart has now become a **predictor** of what would happen if people learned what they say they want. *Have* is the current (prevalence) level. *Have* + *gap* is the future level. In the case of negative gaps, the gap bars are plotted on the other side of the y-axis, (a glitch of the stacking function of ggplot2 or a feature - one cannot unlearn). Note how from a competing narrative of Fig 71, (competing bars), we have switched to a **growth mindset** narrative with the "what if you could learn anything you wanted". How might we use this chart to prioritize what skills to teach?

CHAPTER 6 DETECTING BIAS

with Marybeth Sandell

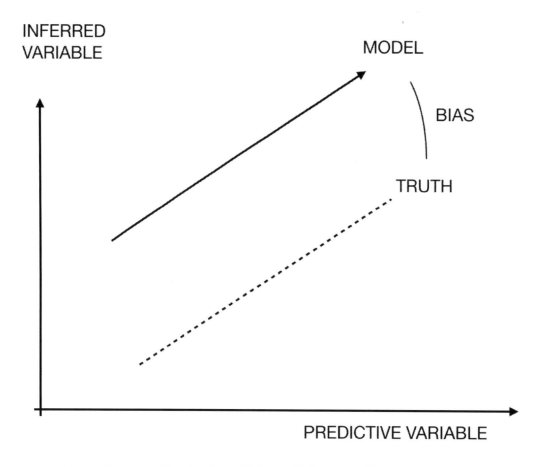

Fig 86 *Bias is unethical when it is unfair, usually against minorities.*

In this chapter, you will learn what bias is and how it can affect a data-driven visual.

HOW DOES BIAS WORK?

Bias not only can be sorted by their point of entry (data, story, narrative) but also by the area they exploit in the cognition system (optical illusions, cultural biases). It is easy to assume that bias is intentional. However, bias can emerge for many reasons.

First, bias can be embedded in the data itself, intentionally in the way it is gathered but also accidentally by not realizing what is missing.

Second, bias can appear as the story is crafted. Again, this can be intentional by cherry-picking from existing data, or accidental from cases where not enough time is spent exploring all data available (usually due to time pressure).

Third, it can be embedded in the narrative itself. Often this is intentional, as in propaganda. But it can also be unintentional as in cultural bias.

Types of bias

In broad terms, bias is any systematic error. In other words, a systematic difference between a model and the "truth" it supposedly represents. In social sciences, bias is judged to be unethical when it is **unfair** (usually towards a minority). See also ethical frameworks in Ch. 1.

Bias can affect the producer of a visual (as in selection bias in data), but also the consumer of the visual (as in *Groupthink*, and the *hot hand fallacy, and so on*). Psychologists and behavioral economists have identified more than 200 types of cognitive biases. Those can be classified into three groups:

- Belief bias
- Social bias
- Memory bias

Apart of the mentioned cognitive biases, when dealing with data visualization, visual perception biases apply too. Let's see some examples.

Bias in narrative

The broadest forms of unconscious bias are due to unawareness and are so rooted in society they usually are cultural (moral) norms too. Note that not all cultural norms are biased but that most norms evolve slower than society does and thus are usually lagging behind reality. Examples of conscious narrative bias are Propaganda and disinformation. Typical techniques used are **FUD** (Fear, Doubt, and Uncertainty) as seen with the tobacco industry and **FLICC** (Fake lies, Logical fallacies, Impossible expectation, Cherry-picking, and

Conspiracy theories) as seen with the climate change denial[41]. Let's see an example.

BIAS IN THE NARRATIVE:
A BALANCED MEAL?

In the second half of the 20th century, a **balanced** diet was assumed to be optimal for health. In school, many kids (myself too) were shown charts with relatively balanced food groups such as milk derivatives, eggs, meat, wheat, groceries, fruits. Yet, other cultures and a few independent research papers show that perhaps that balanced food narrative isn't the healthiest one. For example, the Okinawan diet contains less than 5% of animal protein, no pickles, and no milk derivatives. Their diet would be considered dangerously unbalanced by any Western standards. However, Okinawans report one of the healthiest and longest lifespans in the World.

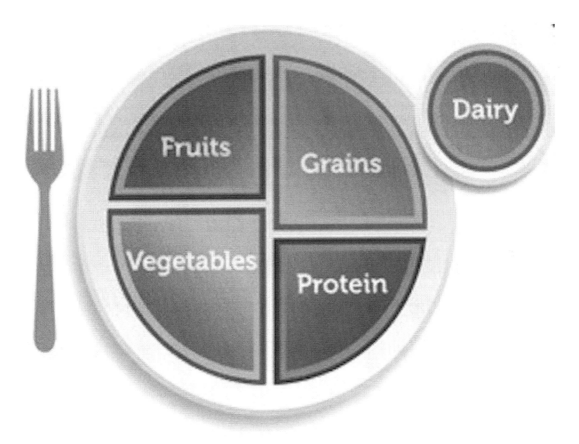

Fig 87 Logical fallacy? How could this "balanced" diet not be healthy if it is balanced? Source: US Department of Agriculture choosemyplate.org

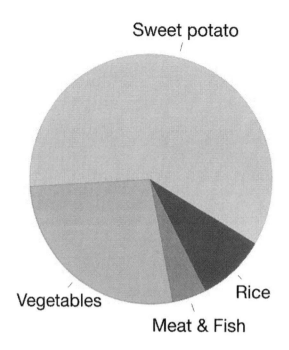

Fig 88 Okinawa diet in 1950 is correlated to the world's longest and healthiest life spans. Does it disprove the popular belief that an unbalanced diet cannot be healthy?

BIAS IN THE STORY: HARDWORKING GERMANS?

When telling a visual story, how the data is used and presented can induce conscious and unconscious biases (well known in advertising and neuropsychology). This can be done through the selection and the presentation of data, colors used, and so on. Let's see an example.

Exercise: Hard-working Germans

Fig 89 is a graph created by the German Economic Development Agency. They used EU data to show that Germans work longer (harder) than the average. But how much harder? Can you identify where is the bias? Time 4 minutes.

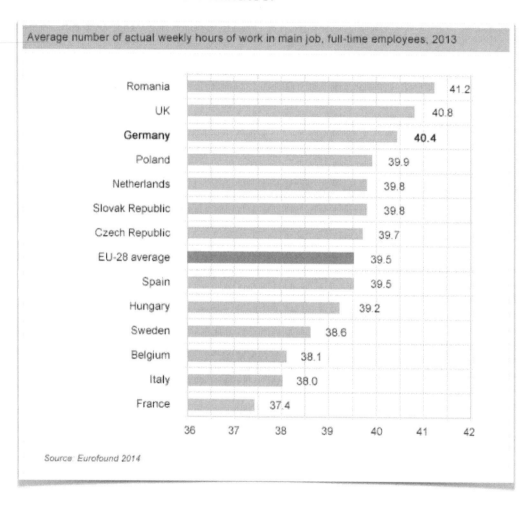

Fig 89 *A partial view?*

Solution

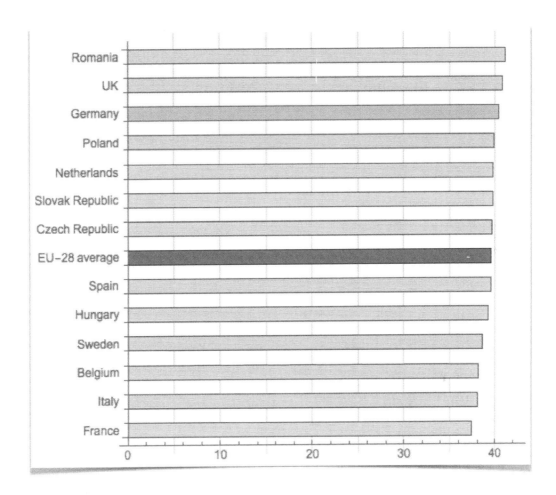

Fig 90 *A fuller view.*

In the chart, Germany optically doubles France. In reality, the difference is less than 10% because the axis starts at 36. A website redrew the graph to start at zero and suddenly, German doesn't stand out much at all. This chart might also suffer from data biases that for a trained statistician are obvious. For example, (due to historical reasons), Germany has more industrial jobs than any other EU country. Germany has more than double the amount of industrial jobs per capita than Spain for instance. If industrial jobs have different regulations or a different mix of full-time/part-time workforce than other sectors (service jobs) then the chart is not comparing apples to apples. The chart just reflects a different job mix in each country. This type of bias is called data **skewness** and it is one of the common errors of amateur statisticians: to confuse correlation with skewness. Let's learn more about data bias in the next example.

Data bias

In journalism, the bias in data comes under three broad umbrellas:

1) selection flaws
2) skewness
3) omission

Some examples include: how questions are asked (as in leading questions); bias in hypothesis or assumptions; mathematical errors and survey design flaws. Let's see an example of a famous selection bias[42] discovered by the student Thomas Herndon[43].

BIAS IN DATA: AUSTERITY CONTROVERSY

Growth in a Time of Debt (2010) was a **non**-peer-reviewed article published by Carmen Reinhart and Ken Rogoff - a former chief economist of the International Monetary Fund. It said that a country's economy slows significantly when debt rises above 90% of GDP. The article was used to justify austerity for the sake of the "common good", (see ethical frameworks in Chapter 1).

Incredibly, a student trying to replicate the results with Carmen's Excel file, discovered that from the 20+ countries considered to make the claim, key countries had been "arbitrarily" omitted in the calculations. Later, Prof. Michael Ash noted another **bias** behavior in the weighting average method used. For example: "New Zealand's (a country of population less than 5 million people) that had one single year, (1951), at -8% growth was held up with the same weight as Britain's 20 years at 2.5% growth (population 60 million)". On a dollar-person basis, that is a **bias ratio** of 1 to 240. The whole story became so comical that Steven Colbert's invited the, now famous, student to the show, one of the students to have ever been featured. By now we have seen three examples of Bias in the story, data, and narrative. Now let's see a few more biases often at play in charts.

OTHER BIASES

1 Confirmation bias

We tend to believe statements and data that confirm our beliefs and ignore the evidence we dislike, (see the previous section).

2 Picture superiority effect

Presentations with charts have more credibility.

3 Self-generation bias

We tend to remember what <u>we</u> say better than what others say. So, if you ask a question during your visual presentation, and let the audience come up with the conclusion they will remember it better.

4 Illusion-of-truth bias

We are more likely to identify statements we hear in repetition as true. Just because it's been retweeted by multiple sources doesn't mean it is correct. For example, the previous austerity paper was cited more than 2000 times before the bias was uncovered.

5 Optical deception

Another way in which visuals can be misleading is optical deception. In 2015, in the paper *"How Deceptive are Deceptive Visualizations?"*, Dr. Pandey studied how such manipulations are

used in charts[44]. As we have seen in the German working hours' example, most of the manipulations in charts consist of playing with axes zoom levels and praying that no one will notice it. Note it is not an excuse to say that we didn't *hide* the scale of the axis, the way Panday measures deception is by measuring what people *understood* after watching a visual, not what is written in the visual.

THE AMAZON FOREST FIRES CASE

Bias can be found at multiple levels. For example, look back at the fires of the amazon forest in Brazil in the summer of 2019. This story dominated the major news outlets for a few weeks as some readers expressed outrage about the impact the fires would have on the earth's climate.

Exercise: Identify potential biases

Apply what we learned so far to find potential biases in the following chart. Time 5 minutes.

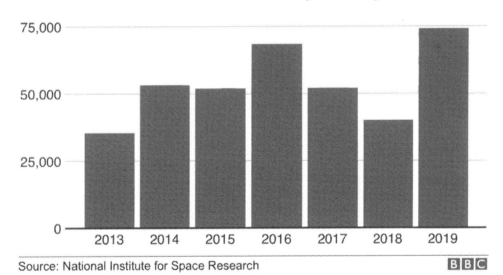

This year has seen more than double the number of fires in Brazil than in 2013

Total number of fires between 1 January - 20 August

Source: National Institute for Space Research   BBC

***Fig 91** Where is the bias?*

Solution

Data was central to this story. Just how bad were the fires? There was one main data source — the National Institute for Space

Research (INPE[45]). Initially, the news coverage presented data that encouraged the reader to be outraged and suspect a crisis was at hand. The chart displays data on the **number** of fires from 2013 to 2019. The graph leads the reader to think that this was the highest level of fires ever. In fact, CNN on Aug. 22 wrote a story that the forest was "burning at a record rate". The first sentence of that CNN story said the rate of burning was a record "since INPE began recording tracking fires in 2013". Between the use of words like 'double' and 'record' and the use of a visual with the 2019 bar looming over all the other years shown, the narrative was set. To be sure, agencies like CNN added to their written story lead: "...and scientists warn it could strike a devastating blow to the fight against climate change."

This year has seen the highest number of fires in Brazil since 2010

Total number of fires, 1 January - 27 August (1998-2019)

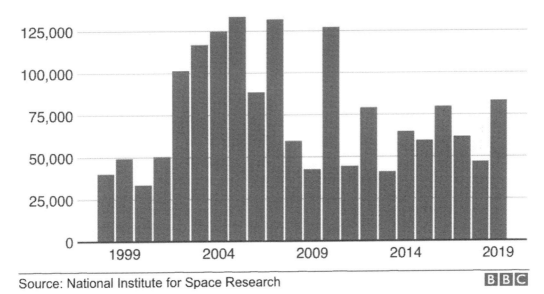

Source: National Institute for Space Research

BBC

Fig 92 *Good journalism?*

However, **a mark of due diligence is to always ask if there is more data**. Often it is there but not available online, or not free online. It may be in a drawer or behind a paywall. It may exist but the time-starved reporter didn't have time to look, or even possibly intentionally ignored it.

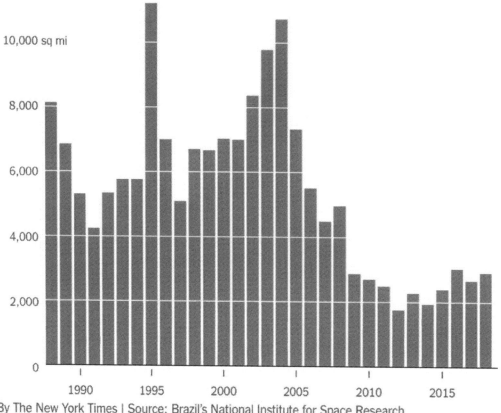

Annual Deforestation in the Brazilian Amazon

By The New York Times | Source: Brazil's National Institute for Space Research

Fig 93 *Better journalism.*

In this case, INSE did indeed have more data regarding the number of fires (it was just not online!). The BBC updated its chart to include more years. Here is how it looked when digging further into the non-online archives.

Still, is this the best data we can get? Is there more? Consider what is being measured: **number** of fires. Does this mean that if we light five small fires today and one big one tomorrow, the total number of fires is declining? Then, The New York Times published the chart below. Here, we have the same source, INSE, but the measurement is square miles burned. The numbers used initially weren't wrong, but rather they were not complete or fully reflective of the situation, a case of unconscious selection bias.

THE FOUR RULES TO CHECK FOR BIAS

1 Pay attention to words

Any good set of data will offer transparency into the methodology of how the data was gathered. This means paying particular attention to what and how questions are asked in surveys or statements made. A red flag is any use of **adverbs** and **adjectives**. They are usually loaded with bias.

2 Follow the money. Who paid for the research?

Big tobacco showed us that the organization that pays for the research can control its results. For example, the egg industry lobbyists are paying for research at accredited universities to promote research that says eggs won't boost bad cholesterol in humans. In the 1960s, the sugar industry paid researchers to produce data that made consumers believe fat was a bigger health hazard than sugar. The list goes on. Next time you see research about health or the environment, try to discover the identity of the ultimate financial backer. Follow the money.

3 Pay attention to the statistical methods used

As we saw, sometimes the data is being selected to intentionally support a position. After performing some statistical analysis, a good rule of thumb is to always ask a more proficient data scientist to find flaws. It works wonders and one can learn a lot.

4 Consider the availability of data

Just because the data isn't publicly online doesn't mean it is non-existent. Postmillennial journalists who were never taught how to do desk research before the internet existed are particularly vulnerable to this bias.

QUIZ: FIRE TWEETS

Fig 94 *Where is the problem in this tweet?*

Answer: The photo is fake. Use Search google for the images to find out that this is an Aerial view of the Taim Ecological Station on fire, in Rio Grande do Sul state, southern Brazil, on **March 27, 2013**. It is not from the Amazon forest fires of 2019. NYTIMES wrote on Aug. 23 about how misleading visuals went viral during the Amazon forest fires.

Made in the USA
Las Vegas, NV
09 October 2024

96511387R00107